THE CHRISTIAN LITERACY SERIES
"The Light Is Coming"

A Complete English Primer-Reader Series
With Bible Content

THE CHRISTIAN LITERACY SERIES
"The Light Is Coming"

A Complete English Primer-Reader Series
With Bible Content

Beginning Reading
Intermediate Reading
Advanced Reading

William E. Kofmehl, Jr., Ph.D., *Author*

Jennie L. Ebner, *Revision Editor*

Christopher W. Ebner, *Layout and Design*
Amy L. Sobkowiak, *Layout and Cover Design*

Photographers:

Linda Meyer Kofmehl
Amy L. Sobkowiak
And Friends of Christian Literacy Associates

ISBN 978-0-9792859-1-2

DEDICATION

This revised edition of ***THE CHRISTIAN LITERACY SERIES*** is dedicated to the first child taught to read using the original textbook. Our oldest daughter, Jennie (Kofmehl) Ebner, was diagnosed with severe hearing loss in both ears at the age of three. Her mother and I prayed for guidance in dealing with her impairment. My wife received the answer, "Teach her to read!" So in 1976, Linda worked with Jennie using our newly published textbook ***THE CHRISTIAN LITERACY SERIES***, opening up the world of print to her, even as the world of sound, in spite of hearing aids, remained partially closed. We were pleased to find that the early lessons (The Pre-Reading Program) helped Jennie learn the structure of the English language as she dealt with the forty most common words in context in sentences. She then learned the sounds and spelling patterns featured in the thousand most common English words. Jennie was "mainstreamed" throughout her public school education, graduating with a "4.5" grade average in her senior year and was placed on the "Dean's List" at Grove City College. As a teacher with multiple certifications in English and Communications, Jennie has devoted her professional life to the Christian Literacy ministry to help children learn how to read using ***THE CHRISTIAN LITERACY SERIES***. Working with her mother and younger sister Rebecca (a reading specialist), she established the first Christian Literacy Summer Reading Camp in 1997, a concept that is spreading around the US from its roots here in Southwestern Pennsylvania. Jennie and her husband, Christopher, made use of the Christian Literacy program with two young sisters they adopted through the foster care system, assisting them in overcoming their own educational deficits. As CLA's "Second Generation," Jennie and Chris are being prepared to continue and expand Christian Literacy, as God leads. We ask that you keep them and their family in prayer.

Yours in the Lord's Work,

Dr. Bill Kofmehl

ACKNOWLEDGMENTS

When I originally developed *THE CHRISTIAN LITERACY SERIES: The Light Is Coming* in 1975, it was intended to be used solely with the twenty-six million functionally illiterate adults then living in the United States. Since that time, the textbook and its supplementary materials have been opening the world of print to students of an ever-growing variety. It is still one of the few programs for non-professional volunteer tutors that can be used with totally illiterate adults, but it also has kept thousands of "at-risk" youngsters from becoming the "illiterate adults of tomorrow." It has been used by tutors with mentally-challenged adults and stroke patients who lost their reading ability, with inmates in some of America's toughest prisons, and with an increasing number of adults and children from other countries who are learning or improving their English. Our model program in the metropolitan Pittsburgh, Pennsylvania area has seen more than 5,400 Christian volunteers trained, and their success is being duplicated by tutors in local congregations of all denominations around the United States. We are especially pleased with the use being made of *THE CHRISTIAN LITERACY SERIES* by Christian organizations in other countries like the Salvation Army and Joni and Friends disabilities outreach.

Three diverse approaches to the teaching of reading furnished keys to the solution of problems connected with the development of this reading program. For the idea of using pictures in the sentences introducing the most common English words, I am indebted to educational psychologist Professor Ken Hill, formerly of Bradley University; Professor Hill used a similar technique in his work with mentally-challenged children. The method of breaking down sentences to reveal the words being taught is the "functor drill" developed by the late Dr. Sarah Gudschinsky of the Summer Institute of Linguistics/Wycliffe Bible Translators. Dr. Gudschinsky, internationally known linguistic-literacy expert, also developed boxing techniques used on the drill pages of the reading program. The work of one other linguist, whom I did not know personally, was very important to this program. The late Professor Leonard Bloomfield's experimental book, *Let's Read*, enabled me to set up a logical sequence of introduction for the thousand most common English words.

I would also like to thank Norma Jean Lineburgh (reading specialist) and Dr. Merrill Bowan, O.D., who collaborated with me in determining red print on yellow paper to be the most successful color combination for the widest range of students with reading disabilities. Since 1983, Christian Literacy Associates has been offering this color combination option. Over the decades, the red print on yellow paper edition of *THE CHRISTIAN LITERACY SERIES* has proven so effective, especially when working with children, that this basic reading textbook is now published only using this technique.

I would also like to express my appreciation to those who devoted thousands of hours to the revision, expansion, and testing of the update of *THE CHRISTIAN LITERACY SERIES*. Jennie (Kofmehl) Ebner was the first child taught to read with *THE SERIES* more than thirty years ago, at the age of three, and is now a certified English teacher and Christian Literacy's curriculum development specialist. Her husband Christopher, our ministry operations director, was responsible for the layout and preparation for the printer. My wife, Linda, supervised the project, drawing on her decades of experience with our own children, grandchildren, and the Summer Reading Camps. She also took many of the photographs. Rebecca (Kofmehl) Pirone, certified reading specialist, and Amy (Kofmehl) Sobkowiak, graphics design specialist, had their input, as did our resident art professor, William E. Kofmehl, III, a "right brained" young man who was taught to read using the red on yellow technique at the age of 5. In addition to this "family affair," we could not have accomplished the task without the work of many Christian Literacy office volunteers over the years, along with those who consented to have their pictures appear in *THE SERIES*.

Special thanks to Sight and Sound Theatres® located in Lancaster, PA for the inclusion of the photographs of a prince and dancer, Lesson 94, and a whip, Lesson 40. These photographs were used with permission of Sight and Sound Theatres® which owns the copyright. Sight and Sound Theatres® is a wonderful experience for both young and old. The live, "Broadway style" performances bring the Bible to life. A ministry for nearly thirty years, their mission states, "Our purpose is to present the Gospel of Jesus Christ and sow the Word of God into the lives of our customers, guests, and fellow workers by visualizing and dramatizing the scriptures, through inspirational productions, encouraging others and seeking always to be dedicated and wise stewards of our God-given talents and resources." Staff members of Christian Literacy Associates have attended many of the productions of Sight and Sound Theatres® and highly recommend them to you. Visit Sight and Sound Theatres® on the web: www.sight-sound.com.

Also, a special thank you to Nazareth Village (Nazareth, Israel) who gave permission to use the photograph of women, Lesson 104. Nazareth Village is "based on solid New Testament scholarship and the most up-to-date archaeology. Nazareth Village brings to life a farm and Galilean village, recreating Nazareth as it was 2,000 years ago." If you are planning a trip to Israel, be sure to include Nazareth Village. You may visit Nazareth Village on the web: www.NazarethVillage.com.

Finally, we are grateful to God for giving us the "mission" of helping His children, of whatever age and condition, learn to read His Holy Word. It has truly been an "interesting walk" since 1973 for all involved.

What Is *The Christian Literacy Series*?

THE CHRISTIAN LITERACY SERIES is the Bible-content basic reading program originally developed by William E. Kofmehl, Jr., Ph.D. over a three-year period in the early 1970's and published in 1975. *THE SERIES* is professionally designed material for use by non-professional tutors. It draws on the broad range of research and practice in education for its techniques, but organizes its lessons based on an easy to use "sample" format. The materials can be taught by anyone who can read well regardless of the level of their formal education. Occasionally, former students have even used the textbook to tutor their own children. The ease of following a sample lesson format allows for the training of tutors in a single four-hour workshop. A tutor need only follow the sequence of lessons and the student will progress.

Because of the difficulties posed to new readers by the English language, *THE CHRISTIAN LITERACY SERIES* is divided into four parts: the separately published *ABC LOOK AT ME READING! LEARNING PACKET* and *Beginning Reading*, *Intermediate Reading*, and *Advanced Reading* sections. Pupils completing *THE SERIES* will be able to read at a 6th grade level or at the level of their spoken vocabulary. The *ABC LOOK AT ME READING! LEARNING PACKET* makes use of a unique "linguistic sightword" approach to teach the forty most common English words, most of which are irregularly spelled. The three sections completing *THE SERIES* rely on linguistic drill exercises, which present the sound and symbol combinations found in the thousand most common English words. Once learned, these combinations enable students to decode any word in their spoken vocabulary. *THE CHRISTIAN LITERACY SERIES* is published using red print on a yellow background. This version of the original textbook was designed to be suitable for adults and children alike, and is especially helpful with students who have some types of learning disabilities, including mild retardation, autism, ADHD, minimal brain damage, strokes, and dyslexia.

The *ABC LOOK AT ME READING! LEARNING PACKET* is composed of 16 simple steps, designed to teach pupils to recognize and distinguish between all 26 letters of the alphabet, as well as to recognize and distinguish between the 40 most common words in the English language. These 40 words account for approximately 40% of all the words that students will encounter in print. In addition to the instant recognition of the 40 words, the pupils will also be able to read in a smooth, flowing manner equivalent to normal speech, thus assisting in comprehension of written materials. Tutors may take a student through these steps as slowly or rapidly as the student is able, but each and every step must be covered in the order in which it is listed. Tutors should stop as soon as the student shows signs of being tired, but in no case work longer than one hour. The *ABC LOOK AT ME READING! LEARNING PACKET* will prepare pupils to approach the rest of *THE CHRISTIAN LITERACY SERIES*, where they will learn the basic sounds and spelling patterns of the English language.

Sections 1 through 3 (*Beginning Reading*, *Intermediate Reading*, and *Advanced Reading*) of *THE CHRISTIAN LITERACY SERIES* require a different approach for teaching the sounds and spelling patterns found in the 1000 most common English words. The linguistic technique chosen was pioneered by the Wycliffe Bible Translators and used in their reading primers prepared in languages overseas. The thousand most common English words are introduced according to a sequence developed by Leonard Bloomfield, one of America's foremost early linguists. The most frequently used "regular" letter sounds are introduced first, followed by the slightly less "regular", and finally "the exceptions." Once pupils have learned the sounds associated with the spelling patterns and letters, they will be able to read any word in their spoken vocabularies. Because of the emphasis on comprehension in the questions included in the *TUTOR HANDBOOK*, the students will also be striving to understand the material they read. The *TUTOR HANDBOOK* outlines for the tutor the following items in each lesson:

1. "Letters presented" – Letters introduced in the lesson;
2. "Clarifications" – Important information for teaching the "Drill Page";
3. "Questions to ask the student" – Questions based on both the secular and Bible story to help the tutor identify areas that need to be reinforced, and to help with comprehension;
4. "Scripture" – A scripture verse or verses connected with the Bible story;
5. "*READING IS FUN ACTIVITY BOOK*"– Lesson reinforcement exercise.

For further information contact: Christian Literacy Associates
Dr. William E. Kofmehl, Jr., Founder
541 Perry Highway
Pittsburgh, PA 15229

E-mail: drliteracy@aol.com
Website: www.christianliteracy.com
Telephone: 412-364-3777

Table of Contents

The Christian Literacy Series:
Beginning Reading Book
Parts I and II

Table of Contents

The Christian Literacy Series:
Intermediate Reading Book

Table of Contents

The Christian Literacy Series:
Advanced Reading Book

A Tutor's Prayer

Dear God,

    Please bless our time together as we begin our reading tutoring. Surround us with your Love and give us courage as we work through each lesson.

    Thank you for this opportunity to teach and to learn about you and your Holy Word.

    We ask this in the name of Jesus, your precious Son.

                Amen

THE CHRISTIAN LITERACY SERIES
"The Light Is Coming"

**A Complete English Primer-Reader Series
With Bible Content**

*Beginning Reading
Part I*

lesson 1

man

cat

1
man
an

2
an   at
man   mat

3
man
mat

4
man   mat
can   cat

1
cat
at

2
at   an
cat   can

3
cat
can

4
cat   can
mat   man

1
man
an
a

2
a   a
an   at

3
an
at

man   mat   cat   can

the man had a cat.

the cat was by the can.

is the can on a mat?

mat   cat   can   man

lesson 2

 can

 mat

1
can
an

2
an	at
can	cat

3
can
cat

4
can	cat
man	mat

1
mat
at

2
at	an
mat	man

3
mat
man

4
mat	man
cat	can

1
can
an
a

2
a	a
an	at

3
an
at

can   cat   mat   man

this can is not on a mat.

this can is by the .

the man is on the .

is he there with his cat?

man   mat   cat   can

lesson 3

 dad

 bat

1 | dad
ad

2 | ad   an   at
dad   dan   dat

3 | dad
dan
dat

4 | dad   dan   dat
bad   ban   bat

1 | bat
at

2 | at   an   ad
bat   ban   bad

3 | bat
ban
bad

4 | bat   ban   bad
dat   dan   dad

5 | ad   ad
mad   cad

16   dad   dan   bad   mad   bat

dad had a bat.

dan was bad.

he would bat a can.

dad was mad.

bat   bad   mad   dad   dan

lesson 4

bad

dan

1 | bad
ad

2 | ad   an   at
bad   ban   bat

3 | bad
ban
bat

4 | bad   ban   bat
dad   dan   dat

1 | dan
an

2 | an   at   ad
dan   dat   dad

3 | dan
dat
dad

4 | dan   dat   dad
ban   bat   bad

1 | dad
ad

2 | ad   ad   ad
dad   bad   mad

3 | dad
bad
mad

4 | dad   bad   mad
dat   bat   mat

bad   bat   mad   dan   dad

dan and the cat are in the  .

is the bat there?

the bat is not there.

dan was bad.

dad is mad.

the bat is in the  with dad.

dad   dan   bad   mad   bat

lesson 5

 men

 bed

1
men
en
e

2
e   e   e
en   ed   et

3
en
ed
et

4
en   ed   et
an   ad   at

5
en   ed   et
ben   bed   bet
men   med   met

men   ben   bed

this is ben.

that is dan.

dan and ben are men.

ben had a bed.

all dan had was a mat.

bed   men   ben

lesson 6

 sam

 sad

1 sam
   am

2 am   at   ad
   sam   sat   sad

3 sam
   sat
   sad

4 sam   sat   sad
   bam   bat   bad

5 et
   set

2 am   am   am
   cam   dam   bam

3 cam
   dam
   bam

4 cam   dam   bam
   cat   dat   bat

sam   sat   sad   am

sam was sad. he sat on

his bed. the cat sat on

the bed with sam. was

the cat as sad as sam?

am   sad   sam   sat

lesson 7

 hen

 hat

1 | hen
en

2 | en   am   at
hen   ham   hat

3 | hen
ham
hat

4 | hen   ham   hat
ben   sam   bat

5 | em   ad
hem   had

hen   had   hat

sam had a hen. a hat was on

the bed. the hen sat on the hat.

dad was mad. it was his hat.

hat   hen   had

lesson 8

 bin

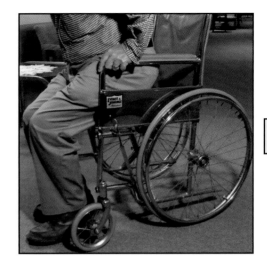 sit

1
| bin |
| in |
| i |

2
| i | i | i |
| in | id | it |

3
| in |
| id |
| it |

4
| in | id | it |
| en | ed | et |

5
in	id	it
sin	did	hit
din	hid	sit
bin	bid	bit
min	sid	dit

| hid | bin | sit | sin | did |

dan and ben were bad. they
hid the bed in the bin. did
sam have to sit on his mat?

 to be bad is to sin.

all men sin.

did   sin   bin   hid   sit

lesson 9

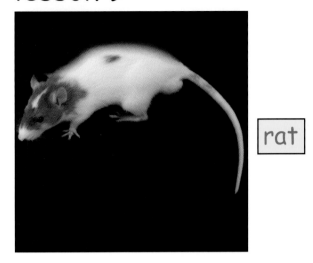

rat

rim

1
| rat |
| at |

2
| at | ed | im |
| rat | red | rim |

3
| rat |
| red |
| rim |

4
| rat | red | rim |
| cat | bed | him |

5
| id | an |
| rid | ran |

rat   red   rim   rid   him

the rat is in the red bin. the cat is

on the rim of the bin. can the cat

rid the bin of the rat?

 all men have sin in their .

can men be rid of sin?

 can rid men of sin.

Jesus

him   red   rid   rim   rat

lesson 10

sip

hip

1 | sip |
   | ip |
   | i |

2 | i | a | e |
   | ip | ap | ep |

3 | ip |
   | ap |
   | ep |

4 | ip | ap | ep |
   | im | am | em |
   | in | an | en |

5 | ip | ap |
hip	rap
rip	sap
dip	map

sip   hip   rap

the cat would sip from the can.

she hit her hip on the bin. the

cat is sad from that rap.

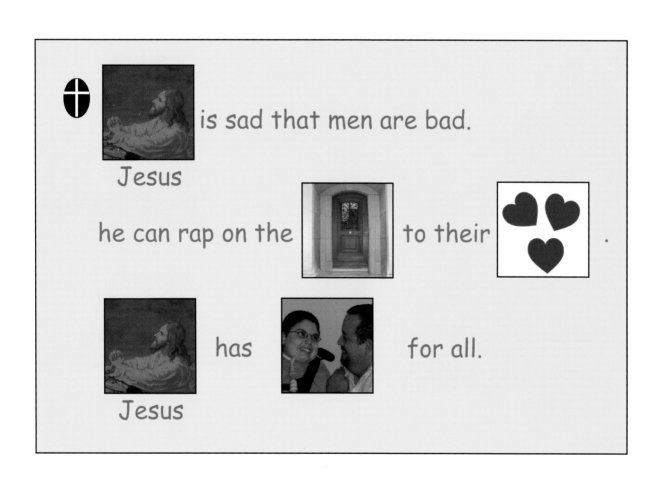

is sad that men are bad.

Jesus

he can rap on the ____ to their ____ .

Jesus ____ has ____ for all.

hip   rap   sip

lesson 11

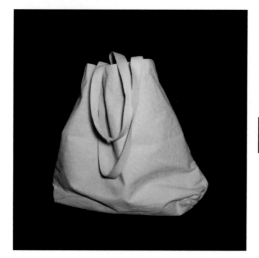

bag

meg

1
bag
ag
a

2
a	i	e
ag	ig	eg

3
ag
ig
eg

4
ag	ig	eg
at	it	et
am	im	em

5
ag	ig	eg
rag	big	meg
sag	dig	beg

meg	big	rag	dig	beg	bag	sag

meg had a bag. it was a big rag bag.

the cat would dig in the bag. the bag

would sag. meg would beg the cat not

to dig in the bag.

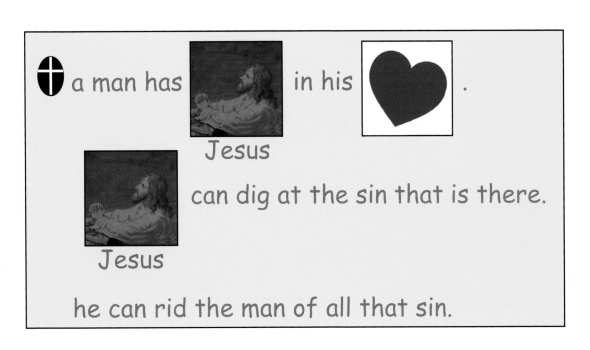

✝ a man has Jesus in his ❤.

Jesus can dig at the sin that is there.

he can rid the man of all that sin.

big   bag   beg   dig   rag   sag   meg

lesson 12

mop

ron

1 | mop
op
o

2 | o   o   o
op   ot   on

3 | op
ot
on

4 | op   ot   on
ap   at   an
ip   it   in

5 | op   ot   on   od
hop hot ron rod
bop rot don sod
cop cot con cod

mop   bop   hop   don   ron

there was a mop by the bed. ron had

the mop. he would bat don with it. don

would hop on the bed. he would beg

ron not to bop him with the mop.

✝ a man can beg to be rid of sin.

he would not be rid of it were

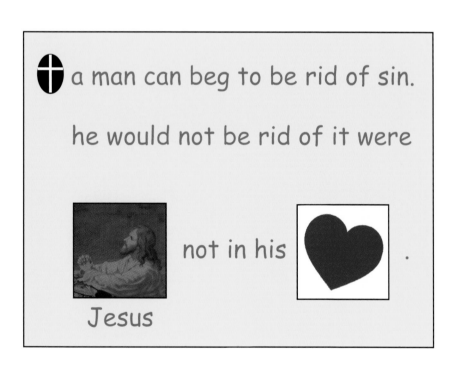

Jesus   not in his   .

don   bop   hop   ron   mop

lesson 13

pig

pen

1   pig
     ig

2   ig   an   et
     pig   pan   pet

3   pig
     pan
     pet

4   pig   pan   pet
     dig   can   set
     big   ran   bet

5   en   ad   at   in
     pen   pad   pat   pin

5   ot   eg   am   it
     pot   peg   pam   pit

pat   pet   pen   pan   pig

dan has a pig in the pen. meg and sam pat the pig. can they have a pan of ham from the pig? they can not. the pig is a pet.

 the men of Jesus had a .

they would pen  in the 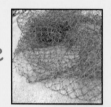.

they would rid the  of bad .

the  that were not bad would be

for Jesus.   would you be one of

the bad ?

pan   pat   pig   pen   pet

lesson 14

cup

sun

1
cup
up
u

2
| u | u | u |
| up | un | ut |

3
up
un
ut

4
up	un	ut
op	on	ot
ep	en	et

5
up	un	ut	ug
pup	sun	cut	bug
sup	run	but	mug
cup	bun	hut	rug
	pun		dug

| up | pup | but | sun | cup | cut | run |

this cup was one that meg had. it was

on the bin. ron hit it with the mop. it

did not cut ron, but it did cut the pup.

there is sam in the sun. can the pup

run to sam?

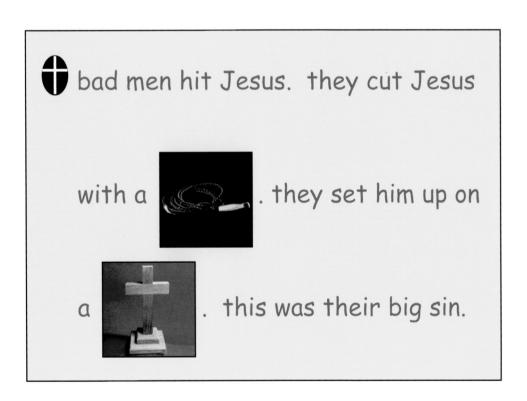

bad men hit Jesus. they cut Jesus

with a ____ . they set him up on

a ____ . this was their big sin.

cup   pup   up   cut   but   sun   run

lesson 15

catnip

nan

1
catnip
nip
ip

2
ip	an	ed
nip	nan	ned

3
nip
nan
ned

4
nip	nan	ned
sip	dan	red
dip	pan	bed

5
ot	et	ut	od
not	net	nut	nod
cannot			

5
in	on	with
into	onto	within

nan	ned	not	nip	catnip

nan had a cat. that cat is ned. nan cut

up catnip for ned. she has the catnip in

the pan by the red bin. ned would nip

at the catnip, but the pup is there. the

pup would nip ned. ned is sad.

 a man can set Jesus up in his  .

that man would not have sin in his  .

he would be rid of all the sin.

would you sip from the cup of Jesus?

catnip   not   nan   ned   nip

lesson 16

tom

ted

1
tom
om

2
om	an	ed
tom	tan	ted

3
tom
tan
ted

4
tom	tan	ted
pom	can	red
mom	dan	bed

5
in	en	op	im	ip
tin	ten	top	tim	tip

tom	ted	tin	tan	top	ten

tom sat with ted. they sat on a tan mat by the bed. a tin pan with one nut in it was on top of the bed. mom had set ten in the pan, but the cat had hit the pan. mom, ted, and tom were not mad at the cat. they can pet their cat.

 Jesus can be with one man and with all men.

he can be with you. he can be with you in

the  . Jesus has  for all.

tom   top   ted   ten   tin   tan

CAPITALS

1.

A a	D d	E e
D	E	A
E	A	D
A	D	E

2.

F f	H h	I i
H	I	F
I	F	H
F	H	I

3.

N n	O o	T t
O	T	N
T	N	O
N	O	T

4.

B b	C c	L l
C	L	B
L	B	C
B	C	L

5.

M m	R r	S s
R	S	M
S	M	R
M	R	S

6.

U u	V v	W w	Y y
V	W	Y	U
W	Y	U	V
Y	U	V	W

7.

G g	K k	P p
K	P	G
P	G	K
G	K	P

8.

J j	Q q	X x	Z z
Q	X	Z	J
X	Z	J	Q
Z	J	Q	X
J	Q	X	Z

9.

A a	B b	D d	E e
B	D	E	A
D	E	A	B

G g	H h	I i	L l
H	I	L	G
I	L	G	H

N n	Q q	R r
Q	R	N
R	N	Q

Ten Important Common Words

Part I

1.
   We ran to the bin.
   We ran
          ran
   We ran
   We ran to the bin.

   we

2.
   I sat with him.
       with him
              him
       with him
   I sat with him.

   him

3.
   We have been with him.
   We have been
   We have
   We have been
   We have been with him.

   been

4.
   Don has a bat.
   Don has
   Don
   Don has
   Don has a bat.

   has

5.
   The pup was there when the cat was on the bed.
            when the cat was
                the cat was
            when the cat was
   The pup was there when the cat was on the bed.

   when

Story, Part I

We were in the  with Sam.

Sam has a pup. His pup was with him on

the  . The pup had been bad when

the cat was in the  . He bit the

cat. She ran and hid.

| we | him | been | has | when |

Part II

6. Who is there?
    Who is
    Who
    Who is
    Who is there?

who

7. Sam will sit on the mat.
    Sam will
    Sam
    Sam will
    Sam will sit on the mat.

will

8. Meg has more of the ham.
    Meg has more
                more
    Meg has more
    Meg has more of the ham.

more

9. There is no rat in the bin.
            no rat
            no
            no rat
    There is no rat in the bin.

no

10. We will be there if we can.
            if we can
            we can
            if we can
    We will be there if we can.

if

Story, Part II

Who is that man? That is Ron. Will he have more of the ham? There is no more ham in the pot. If that can has ham in it, Ron can have a bit.

who   will   more   no   if

THE CHRISTIAN LITERACY SERIES
"The Light Is Coming"

**A Complete English Primer-Reader Series
With Bible Content**

Beginning Reading
Part II

Lesson 17

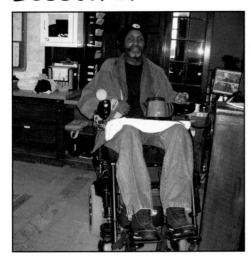 len

 lid

1
len
en

2
en	id	ap
len	lid	lap

3
len
lid
lap

4
len	lid	lap
ben	bid	bap
men	mid	map

5
ot	eg	et	ip	ed	ad
lot	leg	let	lip	led	lad

led	len	let	lot	lid	lap

54

Len had a can of ham. The ham was for him and Tom. Len cut the lid from the can. He cut up the ham. One bit was for him and one bit for Tom. There was a lot of ham. Tom led in the cat. Would Len let the cat have a bit of ham?

Len would if the cat sat on his lap.

A man had a lot of sin in his . He was a bad man. He let Jesus into his . Jesus led him up from sin.

lot   let   len   lap   lid   led

Lesson 18

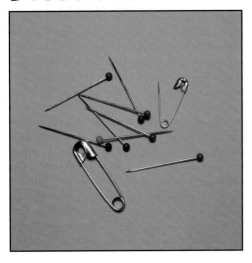

pins

cups

1 | pins
pin

2 | pin cup mat
pins cups mats

3 | pins
cups
mats

4 | pins cups mats
pin cup mat

5 | cut leg bit sin
cuts legs bits sins

5 | bun hit run rip let
buns hits runs rips lets

| pins cups mats bits cuts sins

There are ten cups by the bin. Meg has pins in one cup. One cup was hit by the mop. It is in bits on the mat. The pup has cuts from the bits of cup. He sat on one of the mats and was cut.

 Jesus and his men were in a . A man on a mat was there. The man had bad legs. His legs would not let him run. All he did was sit on the mat. Would Jesus rid him of his bad legs? Would Jesus rid his  of all his sins?

| sins | pins | cuts | cups | mats | bits |

57

Lesson 19

 fan

 fig

1 | fan
    | an

2 | an   ig   ed
    | fan   fig   fed

3 | fan
    | fig
    | fed

4 | fan   fig   fed
    | ban   big   bed
    | ran   rig   red

5 | at   ad   in   it   un   igs
    | fat   fad   fin   fit   fun   figs

fan   fat   fed   fig

Pam was hot. She sat with her fan on the mat. She would fan as Tom fed her. Tom had ten figs for Pam. He fed the figs to her one by one. Was Pam fat from all the figs Tom fed to her?

 A lot of men were with Jesus. They had to be fed. A lad let Jesus have 5 buns and 2 . With the buns and , Jesus fed all of the men.

| fed | fat | fig | fan |

Lesson 20

cub

bob

1
```
cub
ub
u
```

2
```
u      o      a
ub    ob    ab
```

3
```
ub
ob
ab
```

4
```
ub    ob    ab
ut    ot    at
um    om    am
```

5
```
ab     ib      ob      ub      eb
cab    bib    bob    hub    deb
dab    fib    cob    rub
lab    rib    mob    sub
tab           rob    tub
```

5
```
rob
robs
```

60
```
cub   rub   tub   bob   rob   deb   fib   cab
```

Bob has a cub. It is not a big one, but it will be big. There is a tub by the red bin. When the cub is by the bin, he can rub on the big tub.

Deb has a ham in the tub. Will the cub rob her of the ham? It will! There will not be a dab of ham for Deb if the cub has it.

✝ A bad man will rob a cab. When a cop has him, the man will fib. Jesus would not have men be bad. If Jesus were in his , a man would not rob or fib. Is Jesus with you?

deb   cab   cub   rob   rub   bob   tub   fib

Lesson 21

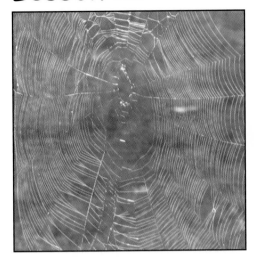
web

wig

1 | web
  | eb

2 | eb   ag   in
  | web   wag   win

3 | web
  | wag
  | win

4 | web   wag   win
  | deb   bag   din
  | reb   rag   bin

5 | ig   ed   es   et   it
  | wig   wed   wes   wet   wit

web   wed   wet   win   wig

Meg is to wed a man. That man is Wes. Meg has a wig for Wes. The wig is on the bed. It has a big web on it. Meg can wet the wig and rid it of the web. She can let Wes have the wig.

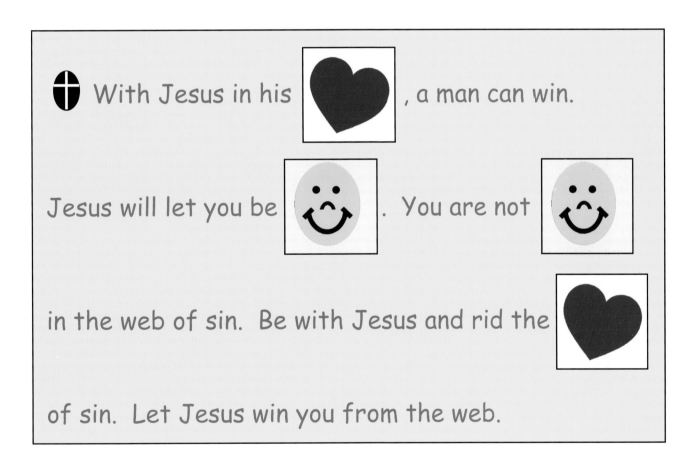

✝ With Jesus in his ❤, a man can win.

Jesus will let you be 🙂. You are not 🙂 in the web of sin. Be with Jesus and rid the ❤ of sin. Let Jesus win you from the web.

win   wed   wig   wet   web

Lesson 22

gum

gus

1 | gum
um

2 | um   ab   et
gum   gab   get

3 | gum
gab
get

4 | gum   gab   get
sum   tab   met
hum   cab   bet

5 | od   ot   us   un   ag
god   got   gus   gun   gag

gus   gun   gum   get   got   god

64

Gus has gum. He got the gum from Len, his dad.

Gus led his dad to the red bin. They have the gum

and a bag.

By the bin was a big rat. Can Len get the rat

in the bag? No, the rat hid in the bin. Gus set a

bit of gum by the bin. When the rat ran to nip the

gum, Len got it in the bag. Mom would be .

 Jesus is from God. God had Jesus be with men.

He had Jesus get rid of sin from men. All men who

let Jesus into their will be rid of sin. They

will be men of God.

god   gus   got   gun   get   gum

Lesson 23

step

stan

1
step
ep

2
ep	an	ub
step	stan	stub

3
step
stan
stub

4
step	stan	stub
pep	pan	pub
rep	ran	rub

5
op	un	ag	ab	em	ep
stop	stun	stag	stab	stem	step
stops	stuns	stags	stabs	stems	steps

66

step   stop   stan

Stan sat with Len on the step. They were sad. They did not have a bat to hit with! When Tom stops by with his bat, they can all have fun.

Tom is at bat. He hits one and runs. Will Len get it? No, Len can not. Tom runs on and on. Can Stan stop Tom?

✝ Jesus is the step to God. If you are to be with God, you can not be bad. You can stop the bad sins when you let Jesus be in the . Will you let Jesus in?

| stop | stan | step |

Lesson 24

skin

spot

1 | skin
in

2 | in   at   im
skin   skat   skim

3 | skin
skat
skim

1 | spot
ot

2 | ot   an   it
spot   span   spit

3 | spot
span
spit

5 | in   irit   at
spin   spirit   spat

68

skin   spot   spirit

Bob ran up the steps. He hit his leg as he ran. Did he skin his leg? He did!

That rap got rid of a bit of skin on his leg.

There is the spot he hit. It is a big rip in his skin.

✝ When Jesus was not with his men, they were sad. God had his Spirit be with the men of Jesus.

No more would they be sad.

spot   skin   spirit

Lesson 25

yam

yell

1 | yam
am

2 | am   es   et
yam   yes   yet

3 | yam
yes
yet

1 | yell
ell
e

2 | e   i
ell   ill

3 | ell
ill

5 | ell   ill
yell   pill
well   will
bell   bill
sell   sill
tell   till

5 | fell   fill
hell   hill

5 | yell   tell   sill
yells tells sills

yam   yes   yell   well   fell   tell   sell   bill   will   fill

70

Meg has a pot with a yam in it. The yam will be fed to Bill. He can have a bit of ham with it. When Bill can have the yam, Meg will yell to him. If the yam fell from the pot, Meg would not tell Bill. He would not let her sell that yam to him. Is it bad for Meg not to tell Bill that the yam fell? Yes, it is bad.

✝ I am a man of Jesus. I tell of Jesus to all men. I tell that God will fill all with his Spirit. They will not be bad. They will be rid of sin and all will be well. Will you be one of the men of Jesus?

fill   fell   will   well   bill   yell   sell   yes   tell   yam

Lesson 26

drum

fran

1 | drum
um

2 | um op ab
drum drop drab

3 | drum
drop
drab

1 | fran
an

2 | an et om
fran fret from

3 | fran
fret
from

1 | trip
ip

2 | ip am ot
trip tram trot

3 | trip
tram
trot

5 | ap ip ug
trap drip drug

drum drop fran fret from trip tram

Fran was on a trip. She had to get a wig. Fran got on a tram. She was not sad and did not fret on her trip. Fran had a lot of fun.

When she was there, she got a big drum for Sam. Sam was sad that Fran, his mom, was on her trip, but he was not sad when he got his drum!

✝ Jesus was one man who did not have a drop of sin in him. From Jesus we get the Spirit of God. With the Spirit you can be rid of all sin. You will fret no more. Jesus will get you up from the trap of sin.

from   drum   tram   trip   drop   fret   fran

Lesson 27

club

glen

1 club
   ub

2 ub   an   og
   club clan clog

3 club
   clan
   clog

1 glen
   en

2 en   ug   ad
   glen glug glad

3 glen
   glug
   glad

1 plan
   an

2 an   ot   ed
   plan plot pled

3 plan
   plot
   pled

74

club   clan   plan   plot   glad   glen

Glen, Rob, and Tim have a club. Sam, Bill, Tom, and Red are in the club. They are a big clan. Their club is a hut, but they are glad to have it. They plan to set up a big hut when they have more in their club.

✝ God has a plan for all men. Jesus is the one who will tell you of this plan. You will be glad when you let Jesus tell you.

Bad men would not let the men of Jesus tell of the plan. They would plot to stop the men. They would hit and club the men of Jesus.

glad	plan	plot	glen	clan	club

Lesson 28

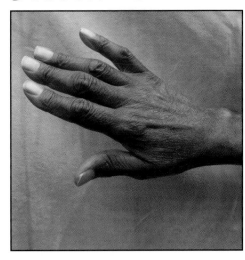 hand

 mend

1
| hand |
| and |
| a |

2
| a | e | o |
| and | end | ond |

3
| and |
| end |
| ond |

4
| and | end | ond |
| an | en | on |

5
and	end	ind	ond
hand	send	wind	beyond
land	mend		
stand	spend		
sand			

5
ends	ands
sends	hands
mends	lands
spends	stands

hand   stand   mend   wind   land   end   spend   beyond

Ted had a rip in his hat. He got that rip in the wind. His mom, Pam, can not mend the rip for him. She will send the hat to Meg. Meg will mend the hat by hand. Ted can stand by her as she mends it. Pam will spend a lot to have Meg mend the hat, but that will be the end of the rip.

✝ At the End, all the men of Jesus will stand with him. They will be beyond this land. They will be in the hands of God. Will you be there to stand with Jesus?

stand   land   beyond   wind   spend   mend   end   hand

Lesson 29

present

bent

1
present
ent
e

2
e   a   o
ent   ant   ont

3
ent
ant
ont

4
ent   ant   ont
end   and   ond

5
ent   ant   int   ont   unt
sent   pant   print   font   hunt
bent   plant
went
tent
spent

1
prim
im

4
prim
trim

5
trims
tents
pants

present   went   sent   bent   print   tent

Ron sent a present to Sid. When the present got to Sid, it was all bent. Sid went to Tim with the bent present. Tim was in a tent by the club. Sid would tell Tim to mend the present. Sid and Tim will have fun with it!

God sent a present to all men. That present was Jesus. Jesus went to tell all men the plan of God. We have the plan of God in print.

It is the . Can you get the plan of

God from the ?

| tent | went | present | bent | sent | print |

Lesson 30

jam

west

1
jam
am

2
am   ob   ig
jam   job   jig

3
jam
job
jig

1
west
est
e

2
e   u   i
est   ust   ist

3
est
ust
ist

4
est   ust   ist
ent   unt   int

5
est   ust   ist
best   just   list
rest   must   mist
test   trust
nest   dust
pest   rust

jam   just   trust   rest   job   must   best

Meg has a big pot of jam. It is the best jam in the West. It is a big job to get jam that is the best. Meg is just the one for that job! You can trust her jam. It must not be bad, for Sam, Don, Ted, and all the rest of the men get jam from Meg.

✝ Jesus is the one who can tell us to trust in God. We will get to stand with Jesus at the End, but we must have the Spirit of God in us. We must not be bad. We must all be the best that we can be.

I trust in God. God is just. Would you trust in God?

best   rest   job   jam   just   must   trust

Lesson 31

milk

belt

1
| milk |
| ilk |
| i |

2
| i | e | u |
| ilk | elk | ulk |

3
| ilk |
| elk |
| ulk |

1
| held |
| eld |
| e |

1
| felt |
| elt |
| e |

1
| help |
| elp |
| e |

1
| self |
| elf |
| e |

4
| ilk | elk | ulk |
| ilt | elt | ult |

5
ilk	eld	elt	elf	elp
silk	weld	belt	himself	yelp
		melt	herself	
			itself	

milk   felt   held   itself   belt   help   himself

82

Meg let us have buns and jam. We had milk as well. Dad and I felt we would run up to the plot of land he has. We had the pup with us. He went beyond the big bin on the hill. The pup led Dad and I to a red belt.

When we got to the plot of land, we sat and had the buns. I had Dad help himself to the jam as I held the bag of buns. Would the pup help itself to the buns? It would if we let it get in the bag!

✞ Jesus can help a man who is sad. He can help a man rid himself of all sin. The man will not be sad. He will have felt the Spirit of God within him. God has held him in his hand.

itself   himself   belt   milk   held   help   felt

Lesson 32

ring

king

1
| ring |
| ing |
| i |

2
| i | a | u |
| ing | ang | ung |

3
| ing |
| ang |
| ung |

1
| king |
| ing |

2
| ing | en | id |
| king | ken | kid |

3
| king |
| ken |
| kid |

5
ing	ang	ung
bring	bang	hung
sing	hang	sung
spring	sang	rung
wing	gang	

5
| it |
| kit |

5
| king |
| kingdom |

5
| send | wed |
| sending | wedding |

| king | bring | spring | ring | sing | hang |

Ken Hill had a big ring. He let Peg King have the ring. When she let it drop into the spring, Ken felt bad. Tom West had a plan to get the ring for Ken. He would set a pan in the spring and dip up the ring with it. Tom did the job! He let Ken have the ring. Ken was glad. Would he let Peg have the ring?

 Men in all lands sing, "Jesus is King." Jesus would have us bring more men to him. We must tell all men the plan of God that is in the .

If men can not have the Spirit of God, they will hang onto sin. They will not be in the Kingdom of God.

hang   bring   king   spring   ring   sing

Lesson 33

 insect

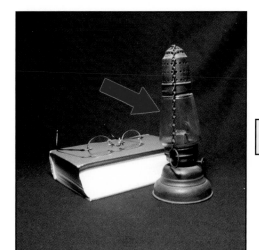 lamp

1
insect
ect
e

2
e   a
ect   act

3
ect
act

1
kept
ept
e

1
left
eft
e

4
ect   act
ept   apt

5
act   ift
fact   lift

1
lamp
amp
a

5
amp   ump
camp   jump
damp   dump

insect   act   kept   lift   jump

lamp   fact   left   camp

Pam and Peg King are at camp. They have their cat, Ned, there as well. They all are in a big tent. Pam yells to Peg, "There is an insect by the lamp. It is a big tan bug!"

That was a fact. There was a bug by the lamp. It would jump at Pam and at Peg. "Get the bug, Ned," Pam yells. That cat can act. It can spring at the bug. Bang! No more insect. Pam and Peg kept the lamp on for a bit.

✝ It is a fact that God sent Jesus to be with us. He would have Jesus lift us up from the pit of sin. Let Jesus be with you! If he is not with you, you will not be with God at the End.

jump	act	camp	lift	left
lamp	kept	fact	insect	

Lesson 34

bank

zip

1 bank
   ank
   a

2 a   i   u
   ank   ink   unk

3 ank
   ink
   unk

4 ank   ink   unk
   ang   ing   ung
   ant   int   unt

5 ank   ink   unk
   sank   drink   sunk
   tank   sink   skunk
   drank   pink   dunk

1 zip
   ip

2 ip   ag   est
   zip   zag   zest

3 zip
   zag
   zest

bank   drink   sink   skunk   zip

88

Tom West was at camp with Peg and Pam King. They went to the bank of the spring to get a drink. His pup, Zip, went with Tom. A skunk was by the spring. Tom, Peg, and Pam ran to the tents, but Zip ran to get the skunk. When the skunk shot Zip, the pup fell into the spring. Did Zip sink? No, Zip got up and went to the tent. When Tom would not let him in the tent, Zip was sad.

 The  tells us of Jesus. Jesus would not have us sink into the web of sin. He tells us to drink from his cup. He will stand with us in the End if we are his men.

| sink | bank | zip | skunk | drink |

Lesson 35

shop

van

1 | shop
op

2 | op   elf   ut
shop   shelf   shut

3 | shop
shelf
shut

4 | shop   shelf   shut
stop   self   hut

5 | ot   aft   ip   ops
shot   shaft   ship   shops

1 | van
an

2 | an   im   end
van   vim   vend

3 | van
vim
vend

shop   shelf   shut   ship   shot   van

Bill Sills has that shop. I went into the shop and got a ship kit for Ben. Bill got the kit from the shelf. He shut the lid of the kit and set it in a big bag. Dad will be by in his van to get the present. Will Ben be glad to have his ship kit? Yes, Ben will fit all the bits into a ship.

 Jesus is at the  of the .

Will you let him in? Or will you shut the  on Jesus? A bad man shut Jesus from his . He robs shops. He shot a man in one of the shops. Will this bad man stand with Jesus at the End or will he be in Hell?

shot   shop   shut   ship   van   shelf

Lesson 36

fish

box

1
fish
ish
i

2
i	a	u
ish	ash	ush

3
ish
ash
ush

4
ish	ash	ush
ist	ast	ust

5
ish	ash	ush	esh
finish	cash	hush	fresh
wish	trash	rush	mesh
dish	gash	brush	

1
box
ox
o

2
o	a	i
ox	ax	ix

3
ox
ax
ix

5
ix	ex	ax
six	sex	tax
mix	next	fax
fix	express	max

fish	finish	rush	six	express
wish	fresh	box	next	trash

Bob and Glen went to fish at camp. When they got a fish, they let Meg have it. She would set the fish in a pan. Ned, the cat, got the fish that were not big. Ned was glad to get fresh fish. He would rush to his pan and finish his fish. Ned would beg for the next fish.

Bob sent us a box of fish by express. When they got to us, they were not fresh. I had to drop the box in the trash can. I wish that Ned were with us. He would have been fed the fish.

✝ Jesus tells us of the Kingdom of God. A lot of men will wish to be in the Kingdom. They will rush to the and beg to be the next one in. Not all men will be let in the . For a man to be in the Kingdom of God, he must have Jesus as the King of his .

| trash | fish | rush | express | box |
| next | six | fresh | wish | finish |

Lesson 37

chin

sandwich

1   chin
    in

2   in   op   est
    chin   chop   chest

3   chin
    chop
    chest

1   sandwich
        ich
        i

2   i   e   u
    ich   ench   uch

3   ich
    ench
    uch

4   wich   uch
    wish   ush

5   ench   inch   uch   ich   atch   itch   unch
    french pinch   much   rich   catch   kitchen   bunch
    bench   finch   such   match   stitch   lunch

french   sandwich   kitchen   chest   chin
    much   such   catch   rich   inch

94

Sam French ran to get a sandwich from the kitchen. He fell on the steps and hit his chest and chin. His chin got a bad gash that was an inch. It was such a big cut! His dad had to fix the cut for Sam. I bet Sam will not run on the steps as much.

✝ Jesus tells us more of the Kingdom of God. Can a rich man get into the Kingdom? Jesus tells us that such a man can get in; but to a lot of men, cash has been the web that can catch us. If cash is all there is for a man, he will not have a spot left in his  for Jesus. At the End, will this man stand with Jesus?

| rich | sandwich | kitchen | inch | catch |
| chin | chest | french | such | much |

Lesson 38

thank

beth

1 | thank
ank

2 | ank   in   ump
thank   thin   thump

3 | thank
thin
thump

5 | ing   ink
thing   think

1 | than
an

2 | an   us   en
than   thus   then

3 | than
thus
then

1 | beth
eth
e

2 | e   a   i
eth   ath   idth

3 | eth
ath
idth

5 | ath   ength   idth   ith
bath   length   width   with
path   strength   within

thank   think   thin   strength   beth   thing
then   than   length   width   path

Beth Sands sent a present to Tom West. It was in a thin box. The box was not more than one inch in width. When Tom rips the lid from it, I think there will be a rod in the box. Tom can fish with the rod. He will have to have a lot of strength to bring in a big fish. Will Tom thank Beth for the present? Would he wish that the thing in the box was not a rod?

 Jesus tells us of the path to the Kingdom of God.

If we let the Spirit of God be in the  , we can run the length of the path. We thank God for sending Jesus to us. With his help, we get the strength to stand up and be rid of sins. Are you on the path to the Kingdom of God?

| path | beth | width | strength | than | thing |
| length | then | think | thin | thank | |

Lesson 39

dress

hill

1	dress	2	e	u	i	3	ess
	ess		ess	uss	iss		uss
	e						iss

5

iss	ess	uss
kiss	less	fuss
miss	bless	muss
	press	

5

ing
pressing
blessing
missing

1	hill	4	hill	tell
	ill		hiss	tess

5

ill	shall
kill	
still	

dress	bless	kiss	fuss	still
press	less	miss	shall	kill

Miss Pat Hill is to wed Bill Sands. She has to get a dress from her mom. Mom will press it for Pat. That will be less fuss than for Pat to press the dress. Pat will kiss Mom for pressing the dress. It is the best dress Mom can fix for Pat. Is it the best dress in the land? Mom would think it was!

 Jesus will bless all who let him into their  .

He tells us to thank God for all the things he lets us have. We can think of God as a Dad. He is a Dad who would wish for us to get all that is not bad.

God would have us all be with him in the End. We shall not be there with him if we are still in the pit of sin. Let Jesus kill the sin!

| shall | kill | still | fuss | miss |
| dress | press | bless | less | kiss |

Lesson 40

 egg

 whip

1 | egg
e

1 | add
a

1 | buzz
uzz
u

1 | mitt
itt
i

1 | whip
ip

2 | ip   en   ich
whip   when   which

3 | whip
when
which

4 | whip   when
chip   then

egg   whip   add   which   when   mitt

100

Meg will bring a box of buns to the wedding of Pat and Bill. She has to whip eggs for the buns. Then she will add the eggs to the pan. Which buns will she bring? Will they be the best buns at the wedding? When Meg brings the buns, they have to be the best! They will be hot buns. Meg must have a mitt on her hand when she brings the box.

✚ Bad men hit Jesus with a whip. Did their king tell the men to whip Jesus? Yes, this just adds to all the sins they had. The men were mad at Jesus for telling of the plan of God. They felt that it would be best to kill Jesus. Did they kill him? Yes, they set him up on a  .

when   whip   which   add   egg   mitt

Lesson 41

 pick

 rock

1
pick
ick
i

2
i	a	o
ick	ack	ock

3
ick
ack
ock

4
ick	ack	ock
ict	act	oct
ink	ank	onk

5
isk	esk
disk	desk
risk	

5
ack	ick	ock	uck	eck
back	pick	rock	buck	deck
black	sick	sock	luck	neck
sack	stick	stock	truck	check
pack	trick	dock	tuck	peck
shack	ticket		stuck	
jack	brick			

sack	back	stick	rock	neck
black	pick	sick	stock	truck

Tim and Bob Black were at camp. They went on a rock hunt in the truck with their dad. Tim had a pick to dig for rocks and Bob had a big sack. They will have a big stock of rocks at the end of their hunt. Bob will stick all the rocks in the sack. Then they will have to get back to camp. At camp, they can check all their rocks and pick the best. Tim will cut the best rock up and set a bit of it in a ring for Mom.

✝ Men would bring the sick to Jesus. Jesus would help the sick to get well. If one had a bad back and neck Jesus would rid him of it. A man with a bad leg would not have to hang on to a stick to get up. He would run. He would thank Jesus as he ran. Will Jesus still help the sick?

truck	neck	stock	rock	sick
sack	back	pick	stick	black

Lesson 42

 tree

 match

1
tree
ee

2
ee	ee	ee
tree	fee	see

3
tree
fee
see

5
ee	eed	eet
free	need	feet
freedom	seed	meet
thee	weed	meeting
three	feed	street
degree		sweet

1
be
e

3
be
he
me

1
match
atch
a

5
atch	itch	utch
catch	ditch	dutch
patch	hitch	crutch
scratch	witch	

see	feet	need	meet	sweet	catch	crutch
tree	three	degree	meeting	street	match	free

104

Can you see that big tree on West Street? It is a fig tree. Sam is in the tree. He went up in that tree to get free figs. He will fill a sack with all of the sweet figs there.

Three figs drop from the tree. Can Sam catch the figs? No, they will drop at his feet. He will not need the figs, as he has the sack of figs in his hand.

Sam will let Meg have the sack. She will fill up a pan with fig jam. Sam can have buns and jam at the club meeting.

✝ The men of Jesus were not rich. They did not need degrees, but they did have the Spirit of God. They would tell all the men they met of the plan of God. They would help the sick to get well. With the help of the Spirit, men would see. A man with a crutch would get up on his feet and run. All men can get the blessing of God. Is there a thing to match that?

crutch   catch   match   need   sweet   street   tree
free   degree   three   see   feet   meeting   meet

Lesson 43

queen

sheep

1
queen
een

2
een   it   ack
queen quit quack

3
queen
quit
quack

4
queen quit quack
seen   sit   sack

5
ick   int
quick squint

1
sheep
eep
ee

5
deep	green	seek	seem	deer
keep	seen	week	feel	peer
sleep	queen	meek	indeed	beer
sweep	teen	peek	reel	steer
steep	keen	sleek	peel	sheet

queen squint deep keep seek indeed seem
feel quick sheep sleep week green seen

When Fran was at the French camp, she had seen the Queen. The Queen had on a green dress and a green hat. She was in a big black cab. Fran had to squint a bit to see her.

Did Fran seem glad to be back from the French camp? Yes, indeed, but she was quick to seek her bed. She fell into a deep sleep and has not been seen for a week. Is Fran sick? No, she just feels she has to sleep a lot.

✝ To God, men must seem to be sheep. They are quick to run into a deep pit. For men that deep pit is sin. Jesus can keep his sheep from jumping into that black pit. Seek Jesus and you will be glad indeed. Tell all the men you meet of Jesus and of the plan of God.

sheep green deep seek sleep week keep
feel queen seem quick seen squint indeed

Twenty-Five Important Common Words
Part I

1. out

   Tom went out of the tent with Bob.
   Tom went out
   Tom went
   Tom went out
   Tom went out of the tent with Bob.

2. so

   Peg was sad, so we let her have the pup.
             so we let her have the pup
               we let her have the pup
             so we let her have the pup
   Peg was sad, so we let her have the pup.

3. said

   I said to Bill, "Set that cup on the shelf."
   I said
   I
   I said
   I said to Bill, "Set that cup on the shelf."

4. what

   What camp were the men at?
   What camp
          camp
   What camp
   What camp were the men at?

5. up
   its

   The cub would stand up on its back feet.
             its back feet
               back feet
             its back feet
   The cub would stand up on its back feet.

6.

about

Meg will tell us all about her trip.
about her trip
her trip
about her trip
Meg will tell us all about her trip.

7.

into

than

More jam went into the pan than Pat would wish.
than Pat would wish
Pat would wish
than Pat would wish
More jam went into the pan than Pat would wish.

8.

them

can

Can you see them by the hut?
you see them
you see
you see them
Can you see them by the hut?

9.

only

Ben was the only one in the shop with Dan.
only one
one
only one
Ben was the only one in the shop with Dan.

10.

other

Will you pick up that present or the other one?
other one
one
other one
Will you pick up that present or the other one?

11.

new

Sam is the new man on the job.
new man
man
new man
Sam is the new man on the job.

Story, Part I

✝ God sent Jesus out to be with men. Jesus was to tell them about the Kingdom of God. One man said to Jesus, "Who can get into the Kingdom?" "Not all men," said Jesus. "More than one will seek the Kingdom and not be let in."

A rich man said to Jesus, "Tell us what path to set out on to get to the Kingdom." "For you," said Jesus, "you must sell all that you have. I can then tell you of the plan of God. It is up to you. Only you can get on the new path."

Did the rich man get on the path to the Kingdom? No, he did not get on its path. He would not sell all that he had to be with Jesus. The rich man had cash as his god.

out	so	said	what	up	its	about
into	than	them	can	only	other	new

Part II

12. Can you get Rob some ham from the pot?

some

some ham
                ham
some ham
Can you get Rob some ham from the pot?

13. It is time for Len to be in bed.
It is time

time

It is
It is time
It is time for Len to be in bed.

14. Pam could hang up the map for Dad.
could hang up

could

        hang up
could hang up
Pam could hang up the map for Dad.

15. These cats are the ones Mom will keep.
These cats

these

        cats
These cats
These cats are the ones Mom will keep.

16. If you have one bun and add two buns, you will have three.
two buns

two

buns
two buns
If you have one bun and add two buns, you will have three.

17. Tim may be out at the club with Ron.
Tim may

may

Tim
Tim may
Tim may be out at the club with Ron.

18. I went to see Pam King and then went back to the ship.

then

then went back

went back

then went back

I went to see Pam King and then went back to the ship.

19. Gus can do all the things Bob can.

do

Gus can do

Gus can

Gus can do

Gus can do all the things Bob can.

20. Peg will pick out a new dress first, then a new hat.

first

pick out a new dress first

pick out a new dress

pick out a new dress first

Peg will pick out a new dress first, then a new hat.

21. Are any of the men still back at camp?

any

any of the men

of the men

any of the men

Are any of the men still back at camp?

22. My dad will be there if I need him to help.

my

My dad

dad

My dad

My dad will be there if I need him to help.

Story, Part II

✝ Some of his men said to Jesus, "Which of us will be first when we are all in the Kingdom of God? Will it be one of these two men?"

"When you are in my Kingdom," said Jesus, "you will see that any man who would be first must spend all of his time helping others. If you would do this, then you may be one of the first men in the Kingdom of God."

What could you do to help others? Are there men who need to be fed? Can you be a help to men who can not see?

some	time	could	these	two	may
then	do	first	any	my	

Congratulations!

You have just completed

The Christian Literacy Series:

Beginning Reading Book.

THE CHRISTIAN LITERACY SERIES

"The Light Is Coming"

A Complete English Primer-Reader Series
With Bible Content

Intermediate Reading

Lesson 44

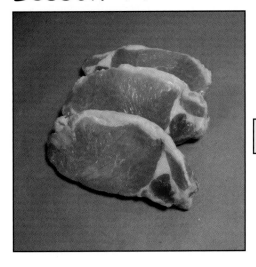

meat

sea

1
| meat |
| eat |
| ea |

2
ea	ea	ea
eat	ead	ean

3
| eat |
| ead |
| ean |

4
eat	ead	ean
ot	od	on

5
eat	ea	each
beat	eat	beach
heat	each	reach
seat	sea	teach
treat	tea	preach
neat	team	bleach

5
ead	ean	eal	eak
lead	clean	deal	speak
read	mean	real	peak
bead	bean	steal	beak
plead	lean	meal	weak
	dean	heal	bleak

meat beat heat seat eat each sea
beach reach teach lead read clean
mean deal real steal speak

Ron Peck runs a meat packing plant by the sea. Ten men are in the plant with him. One of these men can not read. If Bob King could read, Ron would let him have the best job in the plant. Bob is clean and will do anything Ron tells him to do.

Ron will see if he can reach Miss Peg Hill. He will speak to her about teaching Bob to read. There are some desks and seats at the plant, so each could have one. Do you think Miss Hill can teach Bob to read?

✝ Jesus was sent by God to teach men. If we let him speak to us, he can lead us from the path of sin to the real path of God. Jesus spent his time teaching men. He would speak to them on a beach by the sea. The men sat on the sand and the heat of the sun would beat on them. They would not think of eating when Jesus was speaking. He would teach them about dealing with others. If a man is mean or steals we must not be bad to him. We must see if we can help him.

speak   meat   steal   beat   real   heat   deal
seat   mean   eat   clean   each   read
sea   lead   beach   teach   reach

Lesson 45

tear

stream

1 tear
   ear

2 ear   ear   ear
   tear   dear   year

3 tear
   dear
   year

5 ear   hear
   clear   near
   fear   beard

1 stream
   eam
   ea

5 dream   east
   cream   least
   treat   treatment

tear   dear   year   ear   clear   fear   hear
near   stream   dream   east   least

The dream I had was a bad one. It is not clear to me in the least what went on in that dream. Tom was on a bed nearby. He said that he had his hands on his ears and he could still hear me yelling!

I think that in my dream I was back East, in the shop with Bill Landers. I had a job with him, from three to six, for two years. Landers was a mean man, but I can not see what he could do that would bring me to tears. Tom said that it was a real stream of tears. That dream was not fun for me to have!

✝ Jesus was to be with his men for three years. In that time he would teach them all about the Kingdom of God. He would let them see the path to the Kingdom. He would help them be without fear.

All of his men were dear to Jesus. His wish was for all of them to stand with him in the End. One would not. He would first sell Jesus to bad men. Then he would kill himself. Who was this man?

least   tear   east   dear   dream   year
stream   ear   near   clear   hear   fear

Lesson 46

food

broom

1
food
ood
oo

2
oo	oo	oo
ood	ool	oon

3
ood
ool
oon

4
ood	ool	oon
ad	al	an

5
oo	ool	oon	oom	oot	oop
moo	cool	moon	room	boot	coop
too	fool	soon	broom	hoot	loop
coo	tool	spoon	doom	shoot	hoop
zoo	foolish	noon	bloom	root	stoop

food	broom	room	fool	cool
	too	moon	soon	spoon

Meg, my mom, is sweeping the room with her broom. It will soon be lunch time. Ben, Ron, and Sam have to have their food. Mom said that she would mix up some fresh hot buns. She had ham too. The men can each have a sandwich with the meat and buns. There will be some eggs to eat as well, and hot tea to drink.

The tea is so hot that Ben will have to let it cool. He will set a spoon in the tea cup and then have a spoon of tea to see if it is cool. Ben is no fool. He will not drink the tea if it is too hot for his lips.

✛ In the time of Jesus, some would think of the sun and the moon as gods. The men of Jesus went out to teach about the real God and about the path to his Kingdom. They would tell of Jesus and of the Spirit of God that was in them. Do some of us have other gods than the real one? Is cash a god to some who are rich? Do some have food as a god? Is drink a god to others?

spoon	food	soon	broom	moon
room	too	fool	cool	

Lesson 47

train

sail

1
| train |
| ain |
| ai |

2
| ai | ai | ai |
| ain | aid | ait |

3
| ain |
| aid |
| ait |

4
| ain | aid | ait |
| on | od | ot |

5
ain	aid	ait	ail	aith
chain	laid	wait	fail	faith
gain	paid	waiter	jail	
pain	raid	bait	sail	
paint	maid	gait	pail	
plain			hail	
rain			mail	
remain			rail	
spain			nail	

train chain gain pain paint plain rain remain
fail laid sail wait paid jail raid

Rod went on a trip to the beach this year. His dad sent him and his mom two train tickets as a present. Rod laid the tickets in a chest, as he had to wait for a week when there was to be no rain. It is no fun to sit on the beach in the rain. It is a real pain to have paid a lot of cash if the sun fails to be out all week. Rod got a lot of sun. He sat on the sand and went for a sail on a ship. He did a painting of the sea with the ship sailing on it. It is plain to see that Rod did not have a bad time at the beach. Did he think of remaining with his mom for one more week?

✝ As the men of Jesus went out to teach, they had to deal with bad men. Some would raid their meetings and hit and club the ones who were there. Others would chain the legs of the men of Jesus, then they would send them to jail.

Still the men of Jesus would tell about the Kingdom of God. They would tell what a man can gain if he sets out on the path to the Kingdom. Some of the bad men would hear them and not be bad any more.

raid train paid chain laid gain wait pain
sail paint jail plain fail rain remain

Lesson 48

 haystack

 chair

1
haystack
hay
ay

2
ay   ay   ay
hay   pay   say

3
hay
pay
say

5
ay   ay   ay
away   lay   today
bay   may   way
day   play   pray
gray   stay   tray

5
day   day
sunday   thursday
monday   friday
tuesday   saturday
wednesday   birthday

1
chair
air

5
air   air
fair   pair
hair   affair

124
haystack pay say away day gray lay may
play stay today way chair fair pair hair

Sid and I were at the fair today. It was a gray day as there was not much sun.

The pair of us did have some fun on the way to the fair. There was a haystack by the path. First, we just lay in the hay. Then Sid and I spent some time jumping into the hay. A lot of hay got in my hair! The man who had set up the haystack was passing by. We had to stop playing and run away. I think he may be mad at us, but we did not stay to see.

When we got to the fair we were hot, so I let Sid pay for two cups of milk. We sat on some chairs and drank the milk.

✝ What did Jesus say about the path to the Kingdom of God? He said, "I am the way." This means that Jesus is the path we must be on if we are to get to God. Jesus is the only one who can tell us of the plan God has for us. Others may think they can have that plan without Jesus and his help, but they can not. Only Jesus can lead you to God.

pair haystack hair pay fair say chair away
way day today gray stay lay play may

125

Lesson 49

sailboat

board

1 | sailboat
boat
oa

2 | oa   oa   oa
oat   oad   oan

3 | oat
oad
oan

4 | oat   oad   oan
it   id   in

5 |
oat   oad   oar   oal   oan
coat   load   board   coal   loan
goat   road   roar   goal   groan

sailboat   coat   goat   load   road
board   coal   goal   loan   groan

Ken Hill and my dad went sailing on the bay the other day. Dad did not have a boat. He paid Bill West to loan him a boat for one day.

On the way back from the bay, a goat ran on to the road and Dad hit a tree with his truck. The boat fell from the truck and Dad will need some boards for it. The boat may need a coat of paint as well. I do not think Bill West will loan Dad his boat any more.

✝ When we pick up coal we get the black dust on us. If we stay with bad men all the time, some of their bad sins may rub on to us. We must not do bad things just so we can be with these men. We would be foolish to add any more sins to the load we have. We will groan from that load if we do not let Jesus rid us of all these sins. Let the Kingdom of God be the goal for you.

| groan | sailboat | loan | coat | goal |
| goat | coal | load | board | road |

127

Lesson 50

 cloud

 mouth

1
cloud
oud
ou

2
ou   ou   ou
oud   out   ound

3
oud
out
ound

4
oud   out   ound
ad   at   and

5

ound	ou	out	ount	outh	our	oud
around	thou	about	count	mouth	sour	loud
found		shout	mount	south		proud
ground		without				
pound						
round						
sound						

cloud loud mouth south around found
ground pound round sound out
about shout count mount our

128

Bill West was mad when he found out about his boat. He has a big mouth. You could hear him shout in the next room. The sound of his yelling was much too loud for our pup. He ran around to the south end of the fishing shack and hid. He would have dug into the ground if he could have found a spot. I had to set out a pound of meat for the pup in his round pan. I could only count on that to get him back into the shack.

✝ At the end of three years, Jesus left his men. He and his men were on a hill. Jesus said to them, "I must be with God, but he will send his Spirit to be with you." As he said this he went up into the air and a cloud hid him from his men. Jesus will be back one day to help us mount the steps to the Kingdom of God.

our cloud mount loud count mouth
shout south about around out
found sound ground round pound

Lesson 51

owl

saw

1
owl
ow

2
ow	ow	ow
owl	town	crowd

3
owl
town
crowd

5
cow	brown	howl
how	down	growl
now	frown	
bow	gown	

1
saw
aw

5
aw	awl	awn
draw	crawl	drawn
law	sprawl	lawn
paw	bawl	fawn
jaw		pawn

owl	howl	growl	brown	down	town
how	now	cow	crowd	saw	draw
law	paw	crawl	sprawl	drawn	lawn

When I was at camp, our crowd could not get any sleep at all. First an owl kept us up with his hooting. Then a big brown cow was mooing nearby. When she would stop, something down by the stream would howl and Tip, our pup, would growl.

How I would wish that we were back in town. There I could sprawl on my bed and not hear all the camp sounds. There are no cows on my lawn. There is a law that keeps them out of town, so Tip will only growl if someone steps on his paw. Then he will just crawl in back of a chair and not yelp any more.

✝ A lot of men were drawn to Jesus. One man felt that he just had to see Jesus. There was a big crowd around, so the man got up into a tree. Jesus saw the man and said, "Today I will have lunch with you." How glad the man was! Now he could be with Jesus and hear him teach about the Laws of God.

lawn	owl	drawn	howl	sprawl	growl
brown	paw	down	law	town	draw
how	saw	now	crowd	cow	crawl

Lesson 52

boy

coin

1 boy
   oy

2 oy   oy   oy
   boy   toy   joy

3 boy
   toy
   joy

5 oy
   enjoy
   cowboy
   roy

1 coin
   oin
   oi

2 oi   oi   oi
   oin   oil   oist

3 oin
   oil
   oist

5 oin   oist   oil
   join   moist   boil
   point   moisten   soil
   joint   hoist   spoil

roy   boy   enjoy   toy   joy   cowboy   coin
      join   point   moist   oil   soil

Each week, Roy Brown lets his boy, Ted, have some coins. Ted could spend this cash on a toy at the shop. He would enjoy that or he could get down his bank from the bedroom shelf and drop in the coins. If he did this each week, then he would have a lot of cash in a year. He could run to the toy shop and point to anything there. Ted could get a big cowboy hat, a pair of cowboy boots, and a toy train.

When he plays out in the back, he may soil that hat, but his mom can clean it for him. If he lets his toy train lay on the moist ground, it will get rust on it. His dad will then have to oil the train.

✝ Jesus was sent by God to bring joy to all men. Anyone who hears the teachings of Jesus can have this joy, but they must not just sit back. They must join with others and tell of Jesus. They must help point other men to the goal of the Kingdom of God.

| soil | roy | oil | boy | moist | enjoy |
| point | toy | join | joy | coin | cowboy |

Lesson 53

house

sleeve

1
house
ouse
ou

2
ou	ee	oo
ouse	eese	oose

3
ouse
eese
oose

5
else	loose
sense	blouse
increase	goose
promise	

1
sleeve
eeve
ee

2
ee	ea	oo
eeve	eave	oove

3
eeve
eave
oove

5
give	twelve
have	groove
live	shelve
	leave

house   blouse   loose   else   sense   increase
promise   give   have   leave   live   twelve

Beth lives in a house out on West Road. She lives there with Peg Hill, May Eastman, and Pat Black. Each of them has three cats, so there are twelve cats loose in that house.

My mom and I went out to see Beth one day. I had a big rip in the sleeve of my blouse. No one else could fix it. Beth had said that she would fix the blouse by Sunday, if I would leave it at the house. I could sense that she had a lot of other things to do, but she will stick by her promise. I think Mom will give her an increase in pay if I can have the blouse for Sunday.

✝ Jesus had twelve men with him. He spent three years teaching them about the Kingdom of God. He had found these men in a lot of jobs. Two were fishing in a boat. One was a tax man. All were glad to leave their jobs to be with Jesus. They went around the land helping Jesus. He would teach the crowd and they would bring the sick for him to heal.

| twelve | house | live | blouse | leave | loose |
| have | else | give | sense | promise | increase |

135

Lesson 54

gate

james

1
gate
ate
a

2
a	a	a
ate	ame	ade

3
ate
ame
ade

4
gate	same	made	cane	james	pale
gat	sam	mad	can	jam	pal

5
came	late	safe	taste	tame
case	lake	save	trade	cave
date	make	shade	wave	cake
gave	name	shape	became	frame
game	state	take	escape	mistake
grave	flame	sale	lame	plate

gate	james	same	made	cane	case	date	gave	game
late	lake	make	name	state	safe	save	shade	shape
	take	taste	trade	wave	became	escape	came	

James Pound was waiting for me near the gate. He came by with the cane fishing rod he had made. He gave me a nod and said, "Could you make a trip with me and my mom up to the lake? It is late, but I think we can still escape the crowd. Two State Lake is safe. There are no big waves to hit our boat. I can taste that big fish now!"

I had to tell James that I had a date. Meg, my dad, and I are to take the cab to the zoo. We all can have our lunch in the shade of the trees. They have chairs and benches there. James said, "Thanks just the same. Can you give me the name of someone else?"

I sent him to Bill. In case Bill is at the big game, James can see Sam. He is painting his house with his mom. He would be glad to trade his paintbrush for a fishing rod.

✝ Jesus was with God. He became a man so he could help us escape from the pit of sin. Jesus let bad men nail him to a tree. He paid for all of our sins at one time. Now if we let Jesus be with us he can shape us. He will shape us the way God would wish us to be.

escape	gate	became	james	wave	same	trade	made	taste
cane	take	came	shape	case	shade	date	save	gave
safe	game	state	late	name	lake	make

137

Lesson 55

smoke

nose

1
smoke
oke
o

2
o   o   o
oke   ose   ote

3
oke
ose
ote

4
note	rode	hope	robe
not	rod	hop	rob

5
close	rose
hole	spoke
home	stole
nose	stone
broke	those
drove	woke
chosen	froze

5
smell
smack
smash

5
sniff
snap
snake
snack

smoke	note	nose	rose	close	home
hope	hole	spoke	stone	those	

Bob Stone and his boy, Ted, were out in their camp on Sunday. "Sniff. Sniff. I smell smoke," said Bob as he stuck his nose in the air. "It seems to be from close by, too."

As soon as they got out of their camp, they could see a big cloud of smoke. It rose from a red brick home. Ted spoke up, "We can run to the house and help those who are in it. I just hope that no one is in back with all of that smoke." When the two of them got to the home, they were glad to note that all were out and safe.

✝ Bad men had to kill Jesus by setting him up on a tree. Then he was laid in a grave. It was a big hole in rock. A stone was set on the grave. When the men of Jesus came by in three days, they found that Jesus was not in the grave. Did men steal him from the grave?

those   smoke   stone   note   spoke   nose
hole   rose   hope   close   home

139

Lesson 56

fire

wife

1

fire
ire
i

2

i	i	i
ire	ite	ide

3

ire
ite
ide

4

fine	ride	time	ripe	hide	quite
fin	rid	tim	rip	hid	quit

5

drive	line	nine	smile	white	invite
five	live	hire	size	wife	inside
life	mile	rise	tire	wide	unlike
like	mine	side	while	wise	uprise
bike	alive	pride	strike	vine	unwise
mike	pine	slide	pile	prize	tribe

fire   fine   ride   time   drive   five   life   like   line

live   mile   mine   nine   quite   rise   side   smile

size   tire   while   white   wife   wide   wise

140

James Brown, his wife, and their two boys were outside their house. The red flames of the fire could be seen inside the house. Would the firemen drive up in their trucks in time?

"I am glad that house is not mine," said my dad, Bob. "The firemen are nine miles away and the road up the hill is steep. They will have to ride for quite a while."

When a line of fire trucks rode up the wide driveway, five firemen got down from each one. By this time, the fire was increasing in size. Now you could see it rise for a mile. The flames were white hot and it was too late to save the house. James Brown just sat with his wife. She was in tears. He had a sad smile. "At least we are all alive," he said, "and that is a fine thing to be."

✝ Jesus is alive! God had him rise from the grave. The bad men could not kill him for all time. The stone could not keep him in the hole of the rock. We too will rise from the grave like Jesus at the End of Time. All we must do is hear what Jesus says and do as he tells us in our life. We will be wise if we do that.

wise	fire	wide	fine	wife	ride	white	time
while	drive	tire	five	size	life	smile	like	side
	line	rise	live	quite	mile	nine	mine	

Lesson 57

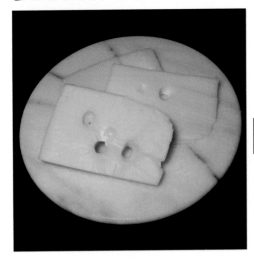

cheese

tom's

1 | cheese
eese
ee

5 | cause praise
please pause
raise

1 | tom's
tom

4 | tom's bob's god's
tom bob god

5 | boy's
cow's
goat's

5 | hundred
method
different

cheese cause please raise different method
hundred tom's bob's god's cow's goat's

Tom's boy, Bob, went to a shop that made cheese. There must have been a hundred different cheeses for sale in that shop. Not all of them were made by the same method. They are all made from milk, but some are made from cow's milk and some from goat's milk.

One of them may please Bob's dad when Bob brings it home. It is a big cheese with a red skin. Tom can have a bit now for a snack and more for his lunch. He could have some on a bun with ham.

✝ The men of Jesus were all in a room. Some had seen Jesus alive. They said to the others, "God had Jesus rise from the grave."

One man did not think that this could be so. He said, "Let me see him first. Let me see the prints of the nails in his hands. Let me see the big cut in his side. Only that will cause me to say that he rose from the grave." At this time Jesus was seen by all of them. He came up to the man who had no faith. He let him see the nail prints and the cut in his side. Now the man had faith in Jesus. Now he would tell all men about Jesus and about God's plan. Jesus said to him, "I will bless others who have faith in me without seeing these things." Do you have faith in Jesus?

goat's   cheese   cow's   cause   god's   please
bob's   raise   tom's   different   hundred   method

143

Lesson 58

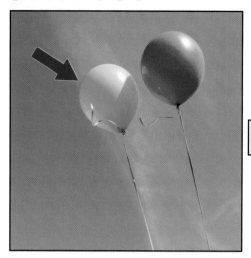

balloon

expense

1 balloon
  a

5 about   admit   amount
  appear   afraid   alone
  around   agree
  account allow

1 upon
  u

5 upset
  until
  unless

1 expense
  ense

2 ense   lain   ect
  expense   explain   expect

3 expense
  explain
  expect

balloon	about	appear	around	account	admit
afraid	agree	allow	amount	upon	until
	unless	expense	explain	expect	

144

James West's dad, Ben, is a salesman. He sells balloons to shops.

Ben West has an expense account. This means that all the cash he spends on his sales trips around the state will be paid back to him. Ben expects to keep a list of all expenses. He must explain each amount, like cash spent on eating and driving. If the men at the meeting agree with his list, all is well. Sometimes they will not agree on an amount and they will not allow it. Just about all of the time, I will admit, they agree about any expense that appears on Ben's list. That is, unless such an expense is way out of line. If it were too much out of line, Ben would not have a job the next day.

✝ Until Jesus came, all men went to the grave with a load of sin. Man can not get into God's Kingdom unless he is rid of all sins. When Jesus was upon the tree, he paid for the sins of all men.

Now, we need not be afraid. If we have faith in Jesus, he will rid us of our sins. In the End, we will rise to life and stand with Jesus in God's Kingdom.

Will I let Jesus be King in my life?

expect	balloon	explain	about	expense	appear
unless	around	until	account	upon	admit
	amount	afraid	allow	agree	

Lesson 59

destroy

between

1 destroy
de

3 defeat
depend

1 between
be

3 because
began
being

5 begin
begun

1 result
re

3 respect
request
record

5 retire
replay

destroy   defeat   depend   between   began

146   begin   result   respect   request   record

There are two gangs of bad boys in this end of town. One crowd lives on West Street. The other mob is from Glen Street. Each gang has between 20 and 30 boys in it.

Sometimes the boys in a gang will beat up other boys. They do this just for fun or to get cash from them. The gangs sometimes destroy things.

My mom says that this week, boys from West Street broke into a house on Glen Street. They began to smash chairs and lamps. Then they set fire to the house. By the time the cops and firemen came, all the boys had run away. Do you think the boys do all these bad things because they do not respect others?

✝ Jesus tells us that we must respect others. We must do to them what we would wish them to do to us. Is that too big a request to make?

If we hear what Jesus tells us, the result will be that we defeat sin in our life. Jesus is the one we must depend on. With his help we can begin to record some gains. Sin will not keep us down any more.

| record | destroy | request | defeat | respect |
| depend | result | between | begin | began |

Lesson 60

flower

sister

1

flower
er

2

er   er   er
flower   member   winter

3

flower
member
winter

5

enter   silver   easter   teacher
number   sister   pitcher
power   under   leader

flower member winter enter number power silver
sister under easter pitcher leader teacher

James East has a sister named Nan. On Easter Sunday, Nan will take a big bunch of flowers to her teacher. Miss Brown likes flowers a lot. She will set a number of the flowers in a silver pitcher in her house. She may send the rest to the home of one of our members who is sick. We all like to see flowers blooming at Easter. Then we can tell that winter is at an end.

Easter was the day when Jesus let us all see God's power. Now, men could see that Jesus was sent by God. Others came to teach their plans for life. They were killed and laid under the ground. Jesus was the only one to enter the grave and to rise from it to life.

If we let him be our leader, we too will escape from the grave. God will give us life for all time.

teacher flower leader member pitcher winter
easter enter under number sister power silver

Lesson 61

 river

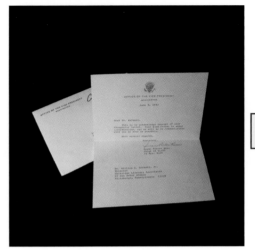 letter

1 river
er

2 er   er   er
river   gather   suffer

3 river
gather
suffer

5
ever	better	dinner	nipper	hammer
never	letter	manner	sipper	planner
whether	matter	summer	zipper	banner

5 america
american

150 river   letter   gather   suffer   ever   never   whether
better   matter   dinner   manner   summer   america

This summer, my teacher, Miss Hill, went on a trip to Spain. She had never been away from America. She had never been beyond the East River.

I got a letter from Miss Hill two weeks from the time she had left for Spain. She said that she liked the house she was staying at a lot. A maid would make up her bed each day. The food was much better than she got at home and dinner was sometimes more than she could finish. She had so much fun on the beach that she did not think she would ever be back to our town.

Miss Hill is back now, but she was in Spain three weeks more than she had said she would be. That did not mattter because she had all summer to spend on her trip.

✝ Will it matter at the End whether we are one of the men who stand with Jesus? Will any manner of plan for life bring us to the Kingdom of God?

It will matter! Jesus said, "I am the way." "No one can get to the Kingdom but by me." When God will gather all men at the End, only those with Jesus will rise to life. All the others will suffer in a fire that never stops.

america river summer letter manner gather dinner
suffer matter ever better never whether

Lesson 62

doctor

world

1 doctor
   or

5 word   world
   worth   worship
   work

1 dollar
   ar

5 collar
   beggar

1 interest
   er

5 consider   together
   however   understand
   remember

5 mr.   dr.
   mrs.   st.

doctor   word   worth   work   world   dollar
interest   consider   however   remember
together   understand   mr.   mrs.

My mom thinks that our doctor is the best in the world. When I am sick she says that he is worth all the dollars she has to pay. I went to see him in May. All the time we were together, his only interest was in me and my pain. Then he would tell me what to do for my pain in words I could understand and remember.

Mom would never consider picking any other doctor and she is not the only one who feels that way. Mr. and Mrs. Silk drive from the other end of town to see Dr. Black and there are five other doctors on the way!

✝ The men of Jesus went to the house of prayer. At the gate sat a beggar who was lame. His legs were so bad that he could never get up. He could never work. He would just sit by the gate each day and beg for coins from those who came by.

When he held out his cup to the men of Jesus, they said to him, "We have no silver coins for you. However, we will give you what we have. In the name of Jesus, rise up." The beggar rose up and ran to them, jumping into the air and blessing God and Jesus. His legs were not lame any more.

mrs.	doctor	mr.	word	understand	worth
together	work	remember	world	however	
	dollar	consider	interest		

Lesson 63

uncle

battle

1
uncle
le

2
le	le	le
uncle	battle	simple

3
uncle
battle
simple

5
little	article
settle	possible
middle	needle

5
animal	travel	devil
several	tunnel	
capital	camel	

154
uncle	battle	simple	little	settle	middle	article
possible	animal	several	capital	travel	devil	

James Eastman and his dad went to see his uncle. Uncle Mike lives about a day's drive from our town. He has a lot of trees on his land and his home is in the middle of a clearing. It is a little house, not big and fine, but it is the best one possible for Uncle Mike.

He has some animals for pets. There is a cat, two pups, a pig, and several deer. The deer are tame, but they will not let just anyone feed them. When Uncle Mike had to retire from his job, he said that he would leave the rush of the world and settle down. "Just give me the simple life," he said. As near as James can see, he got his dream.

✝ I just saw an article about the end of the world. It said that the Devil will gather together all his men. He will gather kings from their capitals and bad men from their houses. They will travel to one spot to have a battle with the men of Jesus.

On that day, the men of Jesus will win. The Devil and his men will be in chains. They will drop into the middle of a lake of fire and will suffer there for all time.

devil   uncle   travel   battle   capital   simple   several
little   animal   settle   possible   middle   article

Lesson 64

kitchen

helen

1 | kitchen
en

2
| en | en | en |
| kitchen | helen | sudden |

3 | kitchen
helen
sudden

5
children	happen	hidden
gotten	seven	weaken
given	eleven	rotten

| kitchen | helen | sudden | children | gotten | given |
| happen | seven | eleven | hidden | rotten | weaken |

"Is my sister Helen home?" said Pam Hill to Uncle Rob. "She is out in the kitchen," Uncle Rob said. Yes, Helen West was there fixing lunch for her three children. They were to be home at eleven. "Rap! Rap!" There they were now. "Let the children in, Uncle Rob, so they can be given their lunch," said Helen. Each day as they sat and ate their meal, the three boys would tell their mom the day's happenings. However, today they were sad and did not say much at all.

All of a sudden, little Tim spoke up, "We cannot keep it hidden forever. Let me tell Mom." It seems that the three had gotten into a real battle with some other boys on the playground. One of the other boys had to see a doctor for his cut hand. A teacher would be by to tell Mrs. West all about it. What do you think Mrs. West will say to her boys? What will she say to the teacher?

✝ Do you think you can keep sins hidden? You may hide them from men, but you can not hide them from God. He sees all the rotten things inside us, all the bad things we think, and all the things we do that weaken us in our battle with the Devil.

Do you think God can forgive us all of these sins? Yes, he can. He could forgive us if we were seven times as bad as we are now. However, God will only forgive our sins if we let Jesus into our life.

rotten	kitchen	weaken	helen	hidden	sudden
eleven	children	seven	gotten	happen	given

Lesson 65

prison

husband

3
| prison |
| reason |
| season |

3
| common |
| cannon |
| lesson |

5
husband	second
thousand	
errand	
demand	

158

| prison | reason | season | common | lesson |
| husband | thousand | errand | demand | second |

My dad says that Mrs. Fine's husband, Bill, is in the state prison. The reason he was sent there was that he stole a thousand dollars. He went into the bank with a gun and gave the teller a note. The note was a demand that she stick all of the cash in a bag. The second Mr. Fine got out of the bank, two cops saw him. Mr. Fine did not fire at them because his gun was not real. He went to jail and later was sent to prison for five years. The hope was that time there would teach him a lesson.

Mrs. Fine gets to see her husband at least ten times each year. It is sad for Mrs. Fine and the children not to have Mr. Fine at home with them. The time that is quite sad is the season of joy and giving. My dad says that Mr. Bill Fine's case is one that is all too common. What made him do such a bad thing? Did he think about what would happen to his wife and children?

✙ Jesus tells us that we must help all men. What we do for them, we do for Jesus. In the End, Jesus will say to us, "When I had need of something to eat, did you give it to me? When I was sick, did you help me? When I was in prison, did you spend time with me?" By this he means, "Did you help all the men around you who had need of help?" Can you say yes to any of these things?

| second | prison | demand | reason | errand |
| season | thousand | common | husband | lesson |

159

Lesson 66

 captain

 mountain

3 | captain
fountain
mountain

3 | contain
obtain

5 | problem

captain   fountain   mountain
contain   obtain   problem

Captain Sam Banks lives near us in the red brick house on Pine Street. It is the one with the little fountain by the steps.

Captain Banks was at one time the captain of a big ship. Such a ship could have a hundred men. It would contain thousands of dollars worth of things in boxes. The men would have to unload boxes at each town. At the same time, they would obtain more boxes to take to the next town. Sometimes there was a mountain of boxes on the dock. It was a real problem for Captain Banks to get all of them into the ship, but his men gave him a lot of help.

✝ Jesus went up on a mountain with a crowd of men. He said to them, "Those who are sad now have God's blessing, for at the End they will be glad. Those who are not proud will have God's blessing. They will be given the world. Those who give help to other men have God's blessing. God will give them help. Those who suffer for God's cause have his blessing. They will be given the Kingdom of God."

problem   captain   obtain
fountain   contain   mountain

Lesson 67

henry

candy

1

henry
y

2

| y | y | y |
| henry | candy | twenty |

3

henry
candy
twenty

5

nearly	very
probably	body
quickly	country
really	taffy
suddenly	pity

henry   candy   twenty   nearly   probably   quickly
really   suddenly   very   body   country

Do you like to eat candy? Henry Day did! It would seem that he never got as much candy as he could eat.

One day, Henry sat alone on a bench. He was wishing he could have all the candy he could eat. As he got up to leave, he suddenly saw something green on the ground. It was a twenty-dollar bill that somebody probably was missing! Henry said to himself, "There is really no way I can get this bill back to the one who left it. I will just spend the twenty dollars and get all the candy I can eat."

He quickly went to Sam's Candy Shop and got some from nearly all of the bins Sam had. Then he went home and ate and ate. He ate so much candy so quickly that soon he was very sick. Henry felt he was probably the sickest boy in the country.

✝ When we pray to God, we may not get the thing that we are praying for. What we pray for may be as bad for us as all that candy was for Henry. God can see that this is so, but we may not at the time. In a year, we may see that what God did give us was the best thing we could have had.

| country | henry | body | candy | very | twenty |
| suddenly | nearly | really | probably | quickly |

163

Lesson 68

betty

family

1 betty
y

5
carry	marry
easy	study
happy	penny

4
marry	carry	study
marries	carries	studies
married	carried	studied

1 family
y

2 y   y   y
family   every   enemy

3 family
every
enemy

5 everything
history
industry
valley

betty easy happy carry penny married studies
every family enemy everything history valley

My big sister, Betty, will be married next week to James Green. They are very happy. Betty will have to keep her job at the candy shop for some time. When James is finished with his studies, he will get a job that pays a lot. My sister will quit her job then and they hope to begin a family.

My mom says that until James is finished studying, life will not be easy for them. They will have to account for every penny and spend just what they must to get by. James and Betty will live in a little home on Valley Street. They can not have a big house up on the hill yet.

✝ The Devil is our enemy. He has been the enemy of men for all the history of the world. He will do everything he can to lead us away from God's path.

At the End of Time, he will be dropped into a lake of fire and suffer forever. He hopes to have you in there with him so he will not be suffering alone.

Will you let him carry you down the road to Hell? Or would you like to live by the teachings of Jesus and be with Jesus in the Kingdom of God?

valley betty history easy everything happy enemy
carry family penny every married studies

165

Lesson 69

 paper

 table

1 paper
   a

2 a   a   a
   paper   labor   table

3 paper
   labor
   table

5 favor   stable   crazy
   taken   lady   katy
   able   baby   april

paper   labor   table   favor   taken   able
stable   lady   baby   crazy   katy   april

Mrs. Katy Bigs is the lady who lives in the house next to ours. She just had a baby named April. My mom says that Katy was in labor with that baby nearly a day. Now I hear that she will have one more soon. Her mom was telling us that Katy must be crazy. Those two babies will have less than a year between them. I hope that Katy will be able to get someone to help her with them.

I think I will give her a present. It will just be a bit of paper that I will leave on her kitchen table. The paper will tell her that I will help with the babies one day a week so she can get her housework finished. Do you think she will like this favor?

✝ Jesus came into the world when his mom and dad were on a trip. There was no room for them to stay in at the town. There was a crowd in every house and all the beds were taken. When one man saw that the lady was in labor, he did them a big favor. He let them stay in his stable! So Jesus, the King of Kings, had to sleep on hay and not in a fine bed.

april	paper	katy	labor	crazy	table
baby	favor	lady	taken	stable	able

Lesson 70

bear

mary

1 bear
ea

2
| ea | ea | ea |
| bear | great | steak |

3 bear
great
steak

5 break
tear
wear

1 care
a

5
dare	share	spare
declare	square	rare
prepare	scare	stare

5 mary
canary

5 there
where

bear great steak break tear wear care where
dare declare prepare share square mary

168

When Bill and Mary Winter and their children went up to the lake in May, they had a big problem with a black bear. Bill had just finished setting up their tent and had begun to break up sticks for the fire. Mary was getting out the food so she could prepare dinner. Suddenly, a great big bear came into their camp. He sat down and sniffed the air as if to say, "I hope you will share dinner with me. That steak seems like something I would like to tear into."

Now, when you have a bear invite himself to dinner, it is not easy to tell him to leave. Bill, Mary, and the children did not dare to yell at him. With great care, Bill picked up one of the steaks and pitched it into the brush. Then he did the same thing with a square of cake. As the bear ran to the food, Bill got a tin plate and began to bang on it with a cup. This scared the bear, so he picked up his food and kept on running. What do you think the Winters did then?

✝ Jesus hopes that all men will declare him to be their King. To Jesus all men are the same. It will not matter to him where you are from, what you wear, or what job you have. In this world, you may be a great king or a beggar in the street, but in the Kingdom of God these things do not count. What will count is whether one lives by God's plan and lets Jesus into one's life.

mary	bear	square	great	share	steak	where
prepare	break	declare	tear	dare	wear	care

Lesson 71

car

arm

1
car
a

2
a	a	a
car	father	party

3
car
father
party

5
arm	art	hard	park
farm	part	yard	spark
far	start	dark	ark
star	march	mark	card

5
hardware
department

car	father	party	arm	farm	far	star	art
part	start	march	hard	yard	dark	mark	

On Sunday, Sam drove me in his car to our great-uncle's farm. The family was having a party for him. He was 65 on the second of March. Uncle Art has had a hard life, but this part of it has been quite happy. He started out working as a helper on the farm for ten dollars a day. Now, he has a farm for himself. It is not too far from town and the land is worth more every day.

It was dark by the time we got to the farm. Sam and I left the car in the backyard and went into the house. Mark and Joy were inside sitting at the table with Dad and Mom. Uncle Art was in the chair by the fire. He came up to Sam and poked his arm. "Well! Well!" he said. "Where have you been. I have not seen you for a year. Are you still the star on that team at State?"

✚ When Jesus was about to start his three years of teaching, he went far away from the towns. He did this so he could be alone and speak with his father, God.

He did not eat for 40 days. At the end of this time, the Devil came to test him. First, he said to Jesus, "If you are from God, make these stones into food." Jesus said, "Men cannot live just on food. They must live on every word God speaks to them."

mark	car	dark	father	yard	party	hard
arm	march	farm	start	far	part	star	art

Lesson 72

arthur

farmer

1 | arthur
ar

2 | ar   ar   ar
arthur   pardon   harvest

3 | arthur
pardon
harvest

5 | army   market
farmer   partner
garden
gardener

arthur   harvest   army   farmer
garden   market   partner

My Uncle Arthur is a farmer like my father, but his farm is a lot bigger. He has his boy, Tom, as his partner. With Tom's help, Uncle Arthur can harvest the beans that they planted. Then they will send them to market.

When Tom was in the army, his father had a hard time working the farm. He had to pay men to do the planting and harvesting. Uncle Arthur spent all of his time working in the garden out in back of the house.

✝ Jesus said that the Kingdom of God is like a man who went out to plant seeds. As the seeds went into the air, some fell on the hard path. They were quickly eaten up. Some fell on rocky ground. When the plants came up, they could not live because their roots were not deep. Other seeds fell in a patch of weeds. These weeds came up with the plants and killed them. Some seeds, however, fell on the best ground on the farm. They came up and had a hundred or more seeds in each plant.

partner   arthur   market   harvest
garden   army   farmer

Lesson 73

 basket

 glass

1
basket
a

2
| a | a | a |
| basket | after | grant |

3
basket
after
grant

5

ask	fast	plant
afternoon	glass	past
branch	grass	rather
can't	last	grand
class	master	commandment
command	pass	

basket   after   grant   ask   afternoon   branch   can't
class   command   fast   glass   grass   last
master   pass   plant   past   rather

Bill Grant and my big sister, Meg, went to the park after class one day last week. They had a big basket of food with them as it was a fine afternoon to eat outside. Meg said they could set their lunch on a table, but Bill felt that he would rather sit on the grass. He likes to leave his boots and socks on the ground and run in the deep grass. Meg says that one of these days a branch or a bit of glass will cut his feet, but Bill will not think about that now.

After they had eaten their lunch, Bill and Meg went past the greenhouse where plants from all parts of the world are kept. Bill asked a gardener if they had passed the gate to River Street. He sent them on down the path to the left. Now, they just had time to get to their next class if they would run fast.

✝ Jesus is my King. I will do whatever he commands. I will give my life to Jesus so he can lead me on the path to God's Kingdom. Without Jesus my life is not worth anything.

Jesus said, "I am the vine and you are the branches. My Father is the gardener who will cut away any bad branch and drop it into the fire. However, if you remain in me and my words remain in you, then anything you ask for will be given to you."

rather   basket   past   after   plant   grant   pass
ask   master   afternoon   last   branch   grass
can't   glass   class   fast   command

Lesson 74

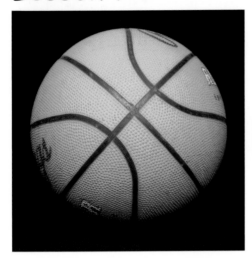

ball

watch

1
ball
all
a

2
a	a	a
ball	war	watch

3
ball
war
watch

5
all	small	wash
always	salt	washington
call	tall	water
fall	wall	
hall	want	
quarter	warm	

ball	war	watch	all	always	call	fall
hall	quarter	small	salt	tall	wall	want
	warm	wash	washington	water		

My dad, Bill Grant, Sam Hall, and I went to watch a basketball game in downtown Washington last weekend. We left our car in a lot and paid ten dollars and a quarter each to get to see the game. Our seats were not as close as we wanted, but we did have a wall to lean back on if we got tired. It was rather warm, but we did not care. These teams always have more of a war than a game and it is fun to watch no matter where you are sitting.

There was one man on the home team who was with them for the first time. Now, not one of the players is small, but this man was so tall that he made all the rest seem that way. He had to be more than seven feet tall. Too bad he did not help the team much. He kept tripping and falling a lot. No one was hitting him to make him fall. Maybe he was upset about his first big game.

✝ In the time of Jesus, salt was worth a lot of cash. There was not much of it and everyone needed it for his food. Jesus said to his men, "You are the salt of the world." We can be the salt of the world today.

First, we must wash away all of the sins we have. We can't do this with water. We must let Jesus wash the sins away.

water   ball   washington   war   wash   watch   warm
all   want   always   wall   call   tall   fall
salt   hall   small   quarter

Lesson 75

dog

cross

1   dog
    o

2   o   o   o
    dog   gone   off

3   dog
    gone
    off

5   across   cross   offer
    along   long   soft
    belong   lost   strong
    cost   loss   song

dog   gone   off   across   along   belong   cost   cross
long   lost   loss   offer   soft   strong   song

Our dog Tip is lost. Katy saw him break his chain and run across the street. He has been gone a long time now and we have not been able to catch up with him. Tip is a strong dog. He has broken free in the past and run off, but he always came back where he belongs. He would just run along Grant Street a ways and then rush home.

We may have to offer some cash in the paper to get Tip back this time. Have you seen him? He is a big black and brown dog with lots of long soft hair. My family will give 25 dollars to anyone who brings him back to our house.

✝ When the men of Jesus meet on Sunday, they sing songs that tell about him. The songs tell how he was killed on the cross for all of us. It cost him his life to take on all of our sins. The songs tell us that God raised Jesus to life. They say that we too will be raised to life if we let Jesus be with us.

The loss of someone to the Devil would make Jesus very sad. Offer one's life to Jesus. Be one who will stand with him in the End. What can the Devil offer to you that would make you wish to belong to him?

song   dog   strong   gone   soft   off   offer   across
loss   along   lost   belong   long   cost   cross

Lesson 76

post

roll

1
post
o

2
o	o	o
post	no	roll

3
post
no
roll

5

ago	don't	moment	so
almost	go	most	sold
also	going	old	suppose
both	gold	only	told
broken	golden	open	won't
cold	hold	over	zero
	hole		

post	roll	ago	almost	also	both	broken	cold
don't	go	going	gold	hold	hole	moment	most
old	only	open	over	so	sold	suppose	told	won't

Today, my uncles, Ben and Sam, are going to help Mr. James Goldman set some posts in the ground. All of the posts that are there now are old and rotten. One of them was broken off almost a week ago. Most of the others won't last too much longer, so Mr. Goldman told both of the men to take out all of the old posts. They will also have to dig holes for the posts.

It is so cold out in the open that the three men may have to go over to Mr. Goldman's house to get warm. His wife has just made some sweet rolls, so they can sit down a moment and have sweet rolls and hot tea. I suppose they really don't like working out in the cold, but the job has to be finished soon. If they hold off on it, some of Mr. Goldman's cows may go on to the road and get killed. Just last year, one of them was hit and the only thing that could be sold was the hide.

✝ Jesus was sitting near the offering box in the house of God one day. He watched the rich go by and drop bags of gold into the box. Then a very old lady went up and dropped in two small coins which were worth about a penny. Jesus said to the men who were with him, "That lady gave more to God than any of the others. They only gave what they could spare, but she gave all that she had to live on."

won't	post	told	roll	suppose	ago	sold	almost
so	also	over	both	open	broken	only	cold	old
don't	most	go	moment	going	hole	gold	hold

Lesson 77

 window

 snow

1 | window ow

2 | ow   ow   ow
window   snow   own

3 | window
snow
own

5 |
below	low
blow	lower
fellow	row
follow	show
grow	yellow
widow	crow
slow	throw

window   snow   own   below   blow   fellow   follow
grow   low   lower   row   show   yellow

It is very cold today. As I stare out the window, I can see a lot of big gray clouds in the sky. Tom says that there is going to be two feet of snow on the ground and we will not have to go to classes today. Too bad we do not own a small snow blower. A fellow could make a bit of cash with it after a big snow fall.

How cold do you think it will get? I hear that it will be down below zero. That is lower than it has been for five years in a row.

When I was a very little boy, I enjoyed playing in the snow. My mom would make me get into my yellow boots and my warm winter coat. She would see that I had something on my hands and a hat on. By the time I did all of that, I almost did not think it was worth going out.

✝ If you follow Jesus you will grow away from the old life of sin. No matter how low you have been, Jesus can pick you up. There is no sin so bad that Jesus can't forgive it.

When Jesus was on the cross, two bad men were on crosses beside him. One of them showed Jesus that he was sad about all his past sins. He had robbed and killed a lot of men, but he asked Jesus to remember him when Jesus came into his Kingdom. Jesus forgave him and said, "Today, you will be with me in God's Kingdom."

yellow   window   show   snow   row   own   lower
below   low   blow   grow   follow   fellow   183

Lesson 78

horse

forest

1 horse
or

2 or   or   or
horse   forest   lord

3 horse
forest
lord

5

born	important	short
corner	morning	sort
for	nor	storm
forget	north	tomorrow
form	or	according
forward	order	

horse forest lord born corner for forget form
forward important morning nor north or order
short sort storm tomorrow

"All my children were born in the winter," said the old lady. "But I can't forget the time I had my second boy. We lived far from any town. Most of our farm was still part of a great forest and my husband Jack had just cleared a corner of it to set up our house.

The morning the baby came, we had a storm blow in from the north. Snow lay on the road in deep piles. Jack wanted to ride his horse to get the doctor for me. Just short of a mile down the road, he found the snow too deep for his horse to go forward. We had felt it was important to get that doctor. But the amount of time it was taking Jack, it would be tomorrow when he got back. So he just sat by the bed and held my hand.

By the time the sun set, we had one more baby boy in the family. He was Great-Uncle Len."

✝ What sort of man was Jesus? He was a man who could order a storm to be still. He was also a man who cared for little children. Men who met him would call him "Lord". Jesus did not fear the power of kings, nor did he fear the Devil in any form. If you let Jesus be Lord, you will not need to have fears any more. He will keep you safe in him.

tomorrow	horse	storm	forest	sort	lord	short
born	order	corner	or	for	north	forget	nor
	form	morning	forward	important	

185

Lesson 79

 store

 door

1 store
   or

5 before   shore
   forth   store
   more   story
   report   therefore

3 course   3 door
   court   floor
   four

5 toward

store before forth more report story therefore
course court four door floor toward

Uncle Bob and Uncle Will are going to open a department store on Court Street. It will be on the north side of the street, next door to the bank.

Their store will have four floors. On the first floor will be chairs, lamps, tables, beds, dressers, and other things for the house. The second floor will have a hardware department and a paint shop. The next floor will have things to wear for everyone in the family. The top story will be a storeroom. Outdoors, in back, will be the garden department.

It may be a while, of course, before the store opens. Most of the inside work still needs to be finished. Uncle Bob reported, however, that they are leaning toward the first of May as the date for their big opening sale.

✝ Jesus tells us, "I am the door for the sheep. All those who came before me came to steal and the sheep would not hear and follow them. These bad men came only to steal and kill and destroy. I am the door and anyone who will go in will be saved from sin."

Jesus says that we are his sheep. He will watch over us and help keep us from sin. Is it, therefore, the best thing for all men to seek the door of Jesus? Will you go forth and tell others of Jesus and the Kingdom of God?

toward	store	floor	before	door	forth	four
more	court	report	course	story	therefore	

Lesson 80

child

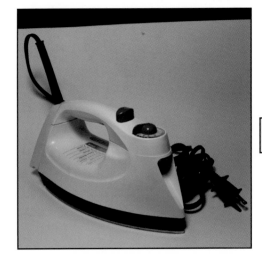

iron

1
child
i

2
i	i	i
child	iron	wind

3
child
iron
wind

5
behind	kind	i	christ
bind	mind	i'll	finally
find	wild	blind	final

3
arrive
desire
outside

5
beside	realize
provide	require

child	iron	wind	behind	finally	find
kind	mind	wild	arrive	desire	outside
beside	provide	realize	require		

"I had a lot of things to iron today," said Mrs. Green. "We were down at the seashore for the weekend, so I am way behind in my housework. You don't realize how much ironing a family of five will require until you find it all piled up. It was in three baskets beside the kitchen table when I started. I finally got finished just a bit before you arrived. What kind of day did you have?"

"Well," said Mrs. Wiseman, "my little boy, Dan, was rather wild this afternoon. He is not really a bad child, but he almost drove me out of my mind. He had a desire to go outside, but with all the hail and rain I couldn't let him. So I had to provide him with something fun to do all day."

✝ What do we do when we feel tired out and mad at the world? Do we act mean to others in our family? Do we go and tell our problems to the lady next door? The best thing to do is to realize that Jesus will provide all the help we need. Just stop for a moment and speak to the Lord. Tell him what one has on one's mind. Let him take on all the cares and problems you have. He will let you unwind. Then he will lift you up and help you finish the day in better spirits.

require	child	realize	iron	provide	wind
beside	behind	outside	finally	desire	find
arrive	kind	wild	mind		

Lesson 81

tie

fly

1 tie
   ie

2 ie   ie   ie
   tie   lie   die

3 tie
   lie
   die

1 fly
   y

2 y   y   y
   fly   cry   sky

3 fly
   cry
   sky

5 by   my
   dry   myself
   fry   try
               why

4 cry   try   fry
   cried   tried   fried
   cries   tries   fries

tie lie die fly cry sky by
dry fry my why try fried

"Why do you have a necktie on?" said James West to his oldest boy, Ben. "I am going on a date with Pam," said Ben. "We are going to see a new show and then try to get something to eat." "I hope you don't go to Tom's," James told Ben. "When I was last there, I got a fly in my tea. And I was so dry I almost didn't see him in time." "No," said Ben. "Pam wouldn't want to go there. We are hoping to try some fried fish in that shop down by the dock." As Ben went out the door, his dad called to him, "Don't forget to bring the car back by 12. I have to be on the job from 1 to 9 this week."

✝ Jesus is my Lord. If I follow him, I will not be in the grave forever after I die. At the End of Time, a great shout will go up around the world. Everyone will cry out that Jesus is Lord. Jesus will be seen in the sky, bringing all of his power to defeat the Devil. Then all of the followers of Jesus who died in the past will be raised to life in the Kingdom of God. Those who did not follow Jesus will be raised as well. However, they will fry with their master, the Devil, in a lake of fire.

fried	tie	try	lie	why	die	my
fly	fry	cry	dry	sky	by	

Lesson 82

 son

 money

1 | son
o

2 | o   o   o
son   does   month

3 | son
does
month

5
done	won
honey	wonder
one	wonderful
none	ton
money	front

son   does   month   done   front   money
none   one   wonder   wonderful

"My boy, Henry, is a wonderful son," said Mrs. Jackman. "Every month he opens my front door and brings in three or four bags from the store. With all the cans of food he brings me, I don't have to shop much. And he won't take any money at all! None of my other sons does a thing for me. I sometimes wonder if they ever think about their old mom."

"Some children are like that," said my father, "after you are done raising them, they never will be home unless they need money."

✝ Our wonderful master, Jesus, is always with us when he is needed. He will help us when we are alone and afraid. No one else can give us what Jesus can offer. Money will not pay for it. Jesus can give the mind a rest from all the cares of this world. Bring the Son of God into one's life! Ask for the Spirit to be with you. You will never be unwanted or alone at anytime after you do that.

wonderful	son	wonder	does	one
month	none	done	money	front

Congratulations!
You have just completed
The Christian Literacy Series:
Intermediate Reading Book.

194

THE CHRISTIAN LITERACY SERIES
"The Light Is Coming"

**A Complete English Primer-Reader Series
With Bible Content**

Advanced Reading

Lesson 83

brother

mother

1 | brother
   | o

2 | o   o   o
   | brother   come   love

3 | brother
   | come
   | love

5

above	coming	nothing
among	company	other
another	cover	some
become	discover	something
color	mother	sometimes

brother   come   love   above   among   another

become   color   coming   company   cover   discover

mother   nothing   other   some   something   sometimes

Today is family time at our house. Mom and Dad are glad because this always means that company is coming. Other than three feet of snow on the ground, nothing could stop them.

My older brother, Ken, is the first to come in the door each year. He has to drive two hundred miles to get home. Ken will want something hot to drink as soon as he arrives. Uncle James and his wife, Mary, will come next with some of their children.

My older sister and her husband are sometimes a bit late. She may discover that her hair is not fixed, or that Mike did not cover the cake that they are bringing. Whatever the reason, they will be among the last to get home, but it will not matter. Dad, Mom, my little sister, and I just love to have all of our family together for another family time.

✝ Jesus was born in a stable almost two thousand years ago. Why would the Son of God become a man? Why wasn't he born in the home of a king?

God wanted Jesus to show men that to God one man is not above another. The king is not any better than the beggar by his gate. A man is not better than another because of the color of his skin. A man is not any better than a lady. All are lost in sin. Jesus came to lift us up from the pit of sin. We must trust in him and love one another.

---

sometimes	brother	something	come	some	love
other	above	nothing	among	mother	another
discover	become	cover	color	company	coming

197

Lesson 84

flood

young

3 | flood
blood

1 | young
ou

2 | ou   ou   ou
young   cousin   double

3 | young
cousin
double

5 | country   touch
couple   trouble
famous
southern

5 | no
noah

flood   blood   young   cousin   double   country
couple   famous   southern   touch   trouble

There was a story on TV a couple of weeks ago about a big flood in the southern part of the country. My cousin, Len Young, lives there. He sent me a letter to tell of all the trouble they had. "Dear Bob," he said, "We all have really had a bad time for nearly a week. All the roads were covered with water and the power lines were cut. Our farm was out of touch with the outside world until the water went down last Sunday.

When we did get to drive into town, we found that some other families had double our problems. They had lost their cows when the flood first hit. Others could not get food to the animals. The cows and their young were on little hills with water all around them. I hear that the TV showed our troubles all over the country. I hope we never get another flood to make us famous." The end of his letter said, "Love to all, Len."

✝ In the beginning, God made the world and everything in it. After years had passed, God saw that almost all the men in the world were bad. They loved gods of stone. They prayed to the sun and moon. They stole from each other and had blood on their hands from killing their brothers.

Only one man named Noah and his family loved God. So God sent a great flood to destroy all the bad men. Noah and his family were saved by staying in an ark, which God had told Noah to make. An ark is something like a big covered boat. Noah led two of every animal in the world into the ark with him.

When the waters went down, they all came out of the ark. Noah thanked God for saving his family. God told Noah that the world would not be destroyed by water another time.

| trouble | flood | touch | blood | southern | young |
| famous | cousin | couple | double | country | |

Lesson 85

pull

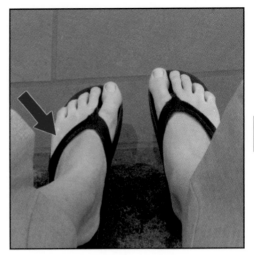

foot

1 pull
u

2 u   u   u
pull   put   full

3 pull
put
full

5 push

1 foot
oo

2 oo   oo   oo
foot   cook   wood

3 foot
cook
wood

5 book   stood
good   took
look   poor

pull   put   full   push   foot   cook   wood
book   good   look   stood   took   poor

There is a poor old man who lives in a wood shack by the town dump. The shack looks like a good strong wind could push it down, but it has stood for years.

Old Sam Cook, the man who lives in it, looks a lot like his shack. The years have not been kind to Sam. He is bent over and has a cane. He wears an old coat and pants that are full of holes. My sister, Betty, says he put the coat and pants on for his wedding 50 years ago. That day, a man driving a car killed Sam's wife and Sam took it very badly. For awhile he just sat and drank in his room. When he couldn't pay for his home, he found this shack and he has lived there from that time on.

Sam won't let a lot of men set foot in his home, but he likes my father and me to come to see him. When I pull open his door, Sam will put down the book he is always reading. He will smile and come over to take my hand and then my father's hand.

✠ Noah and his family loved God, but some of their children and their grandchildren did not. They became just as bad as the men who lived before the flood.

God tried to help them by giving them a set of laws to live by. These laws are called the Ten Commandments. The Ten Commandments tell us not to lie and steal. They tell us that we must not love the gods of stone and wood. We must not try to take another man's wife from him or want to take the things he owns. These laws are still as good today as they were thousands of years ago, when God gave them.

poor	pull	took	put	stood	full	look
push	good	foot	book	cook	wood	

201

Lesson 86

bird

girl

1 bird
   ir

2 ir   ir   ir
   bird   girl   first

3 bird
   girl
   first

5 sir
   third
   thirty
   birth

5 jen   pen
   jennie   pennies

bird   girl   first   sir   third   thirty

Jennie, the little girl next door, has a yellow bird she keeps in a small coop. One day, as she was cleaning the coop, the bird got out. First it would just fly around the room. Then it saw a window and went outside. The little girl ran out of her house. She was crying, because she did not think she would see the yellow bird anymore. The thirty-year-old man who lives across the street saw her. "Why are you crying, Jennie?" he asked.

"Please, sir!" she called to him. "Did you see my little yellow bird? I saw him fly out of his coop."

"There he is in the pine tree," said Mr. Spring. "Bring out the coop with some food inside and the bird may go back in." They tried two times to get the bird into the coop and failed. Finally, on the third try, they got him in. Then Jennie shut the coop door before he could fly out.

✝ The Ten Commandments are good laws to live by, but they will not save men from the pit of sin. If someone were able to follow all of the commandments every day of his life, he still would not be free from sin. Only those who are free of sin can enter God's Kingdom.

How then can anyone get into the Kingdom? The only way is to let Jesus into one's life. If you do, the blood of Jesus on the cross will wash away all sins. Jesus died on the cross to pay for all of the sins of men. You must trust in him and let him lead you. Then you will be able to enter the Kingdom of God.

---

thirty   bird   third   girl   sir   first

Lesson 87

earth

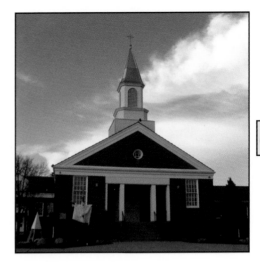

church

1 earth
ear

2 early   earn
heard   pearl
learn   earl

1 her
er

5 perhaps   serve   deserve
person   servant   preserve

1 church
ur

2 ur   ur   ur
church   burn   purpose

3 church
burn
purpose

5 hurry   surprise
hurt   turn
return   further

earth   early   heard   learn   her   perhaps
person   serve   church   burn   purpose   hurry
hurt   return   surprise   turn   further

204

"Have you heard?" said Bill West to Bob Bigs. "There is a church over on Pine Street where a person can learn to read in the summertime!" "How much do they make you pay?" asked Bob. "Not one penny," said Bill. That was a real surprise to me, too. Joy King went there to see if they could help her. She is in a hurry to learn, so she will return to meet with her teacher three times a week. Joy told me her teacher's purpose in teaching is to serve Jesus further."

"Perhaps there will be a teacher at that church who would work with me," said Bob, as he went out the door. "It won't hurt to ask," called Bill, "just try to get there early."

✝ At the End of Time, all the men of Earth will pass before God. If a person's name is written in the Book of Life, he or she will be a part of God's Kingdom. Anyone who is not listed in that Book belongs to the Devil. The Devil and his followers are to be put into a lake of fire which will burn forever.

When a person's turn comes, will their name be in the Book of Life? It will be, if they let Jesus be King in their life. Could Jesus be the King for you, or will it be the Devil?

turn	earth	surprise	early	return	heard
further	hurt	learn	hurry	her	purpose
perhaps	burn	person	church	serve	

Lesson 88

 ruth

 pupil

1
ruth
uth
u

2
u   u   u
ruth   blue   include

3
ruth
blue
include

5
rule
true
truth

1
pupil
pu
u

2
u   u   u
pupil   human   use

3
pupil
human
use

5
continue
figure
refuse
music

ruth pupil music blue continue figure human
include refuse rule true truth use

Ruth Jackson is a widow. Her husband died several years ago. Mrs. Jackson earns money by giving music lessons in her home. My sister, Mary, has been her pupil for two years. When Dad lost his job last month, he felt that Mary's lessons would have to stop. My mom and dad could not figure how they could include them when no money was coming in. When Mrs. Jackson heard of our problem, she refused to let Mary quit. "That girl has a lot of promise," she said. "It would be sad for her not to use it. As long as you are out of work, Mary can come and have free lessons."

Well, Dad and Mom make it a rule not to take that kind of help from a person unless they can help him in some way. So they found out that Mrs. Jackson's music room needed painting. She got the paint and our family did the work with brushes. Now she has a room that is a pale shade of blue, and Mary has her lessons.

✝ It is very hard to live as God would want us to. We are all human, and the truth is that we have sin in us from the day we are born. It is also true that the Devil is always glad to pull us toward him.

If we had to battle sin on our own every day, I don't think we would win. However, we are not on our own if we ask Jesus into our lives. He will be with you at all times. Ask him to help you whenever you feel the Devil is pulling at you. Use his strength as the battle with sin continues!

use	ruth	truth	pupil	true	music	rule
blue	refuse	continue	include	figure	human	

Lesson 89

 stuart

 new york

1 | stuart
u

5 | during
due
duty

1 | new york
new
ew

5 | few   new
flew   news
grew   stew
threw blew

stuart   during   due   duty   few
flew   grew   new   news

Stuart Cook is one of my cousins. His father is in the army, and his family has lived in countries around the world. During their last trip back to the States, they flew into New York. Stuart says that when you come into a country you must tell what you have in all the bags. If you have just a few dollars worth of presents, they will let you by. If you have a lot, then a duty is due and you pay it before you can get the bags. They will also check bags for drugs, guns, and other things you can't bring into the country.

Stuart says that the man in front of him was checked very closely. It seemed that he grew more upset every second. When some drugs were found hidden in his bag, you could figure why he had been upset! Stuart said that his father just read in the newpaper that the man was sent to jail for years.

✝ Some of the bad men in Jesus' time tried to find ways to trick him. One time, they asked him about paying taxes to the king. They figured that if he said "no," the king would kill him. If he said "yes," the crowd would be mad because they did not like the king. Jesus told them to show him a coin. "Who is that on this coin?" he asked.

"It looks like the king," said the bad men. "Then give to the king that which is his," Jesus said, "and give to God what is God's."

news	stuart	new	during	grew
	due	flew	duty	few

209

Lesson 90

bread

head

1
bread
ead
ea

2
ea	ea	ea
bread	head	weather

3
bread
head
weather

5
already	heaven	pleasant
dead	heavy	read
deaf	instead	ready
death	jealous	spread
health	thread	threaten

bread health weather already dead deaf
death head heaven heavy instead jealous
pleasant read ready spread threaten

We just got a note from my older brother. He said, "We have had very bad weather the past few weeks. It has been cold with heavy rains. Weather like this is bad for my health. My nose is all clogged now. I think I have a head cold and I am already deaf in my left ear. The doctor says a new bug threatens to spread in this town. He gave me a shot so my body would be ready for it. Getting a shot is not pleasant, but I think I would rather take that instead of the bug.

Doctor Young told me to get lots of sleep. Lately, I have been dead tired all the time. My wife will be glad for me to stay home more. I think she has been jealous of the time I spend on my work. Now she will be happy to make some bread and bring me a cup of tea in bed." We always like to get notes from my brother. I think I will pray for him to get well.

✝ I read the other day that Jesus said, "I am the Bread of Life." This means that we must live on the words of Jesus, not just on the bread we can get in a store.

If Jesus has led us and has been a part of us, we need have no fear of death. For after this body on Earth is gone, we will go to Heaven and be even closer to our Lord Jesus.

threaten   bread   spread   health   ready   weather
read   already   pleasant   dead   deaf   jealous
death   instead   head   heavy   heaven

Lesson 91

steve

hero

1
| steve |
| eve |
| e |

2
e		e		e
steve		be		these

3
| steve |
| be |
| these |

5
even	jesus
evening	me
evil	secret
we	she
idea	peter

1
| hero |
| e |

5
| he |
| here |

steve	be	these	even	evening	evil	he
idea	jesus	me	secret	peter	hero	

"My older brother, Steve, was a real hero Sunday evening," Peter Hill said to me. "He was coming home from work when he saw a car slide off the road and into a tree. Steve pulled to the side of the road and went back to see if he could be of help. A man lay on the front seat and two children were in the back. Just as he opened the door, Steve saw smoke rising from the floor of the car. He pulled the man out and carried him away from the wreck. When he went back for the children, the fire had gotten even more of a start. My brother just got the children away before the car went up in flames."

✝ Do you have any idea who the king of this world is? He has tried to keep this fact a secret for many years, but all the followers of Jesus can tell you his name. He is the Devil. If you want to see that he is king, just look at the newspaper or watch TV. Everywhere the power of evil seems to be on the rise.

The Lord Jesus and his men spoke of our time. The Devil is trying very had to make us all his followers, for soon the last battle will begin here between him and Jesus. Which side do you want to be on in these final days? You must be on one side or the other. No one will be able to just sit on the sidelines and watch.

steve	be	hero	these	peter	even	secret
	evening	me	evil	he	jesus	idea

Lesson 92

 cent

 circus

1

cent
ent

3

cent
circus
certain

5

center	december
certainly	decide
circle	necessary
city	

cent	circus	certain	center	certainly
circle	city	december	decide	necessary

Dad was speaking to my uncle and said, "The Wonder Brothers Circus will be in the city in early December. Every year, they put on a week of shows at the Fairgrounds. It would certainly be a lot of fun to see, but I can't decide if our family will go this time.

Everything costs so much these days. Each ticket has gone up 50 cents over what it was last year. I am certain we could find something a lot more necessary to our lives to spend thirty dollars on, but the children will be so sad if they don't go.

Bill will be ten during that week and he always thinks the circus comes to town just for him. It is so hard to decide. My mind just keeps going around in a circle. What do you think I need to do?"

✝ Jesus needs to be the center of our life. If he is, we can be certain that he will help us any time we are in trouble. Jesus told us how to speak to God in our prayers.

One prayer he gave us to use is called the Lord's Prayer. We need to pray something like this to our Father in Heaven, "May God's name be important. May God's Kingdom come. May God's will be done on earth as it is in Heaven. Give us our food for today. Forgive us for the bad things we have done, the way we forgive those who have done bad things to us. Do not test us. Please help us, so that we will not do evil things. The Kingdom and power and praise belong to you forever."

necessary	cent	decide	circus	december
certain	city	center	circle	certainly

215

Lesson 93

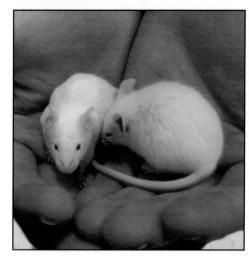

mice

bracelet

1
mice
ice
i

3
mice
force
place

5

alice	notice	race
bracelet	office	service
experience	price	space
face	peace	voice
ice	practice	
nice		

mice   force   place   alice   bracelet   face
ice   nice   notice   office   price   peace
practice   race   service   space   voice

My mom told my dad, "Today was Alice Sanders' birthday. The girls in her office gave a party for her after work. Everyone in the service department came too, so the place was really crowded. I wish you could have seen Alice's face! The party was a real suprise for her. She had no notice at all of what was planned, so she had been about to leave for home. One of the girls had to race after her and almost forced her to wait.

It was a very nice party. There was cake and ice cream, tea and soft drinks. The presents for Alice took up all the space on her desk. The one she liked best was a bracelet with two little gold mice on it. You could tell by Alice's voice as she thanked everyone that she really was pleased with her surprise party."

✝ Everyday in the newspapers we read of men who are trying to bring peace to the world. However, whenever they stop a war in one part of the world, another always starts somewhere else.

There will never be peace for all men until everyone is ruled by Jesus and practices his teachings. There are men who have not even been told the story of Jesus. They have not been asked to decide which path they will follow. Every day we fail to tell others about Jesus, the world pays a price. Thousands of men die in sin. More men in every country on earth continue to want to kill each other.

Do you want to work for peace? Win one other person to Jesus, and we will be one step closer to that goal.

voice   mice   space   force   service   place
race   alice   practice   bracelet   peace
face   price   ice   office   nice   notice

217

Lesson 94

prince

dancer

1
| prince |
| ince |
| in |

3
| prince |
| officer |
| chance |

5
advance	except
dance	france
dancer	once
difference	produce
distance	since

prince   officer   chance   advance   dance
dancer   difference   distance   except
france   once   produce   since

I was sick in bed for three days last week. Since my mom hadn't had a chance to get me any new books, there was nothing to do except watch TV. Watching daytime TV is more painful than being sick. It really makes no difference where you turn to, for they are all just as bad. One had a play that was produced in France. It was about an army officer who was once a prince. He didn't act like any officer I ever saw. It seemed like he was singing or in a dance most of the time. The plot couldn't advance at all without dancers jumping all over the place and singing at each other. As sick as I was, I finally was able to get out of bed, crawl the short distance to the TV set, and shut it off.

✝ Jesus has been called the Prince of Peace. He can bring peace to all who hear his words. How will men in all parts of the world learn the words of Jesus? If we cannot go, we must help send others.

Churches have been sending out teachers to tell of the Good News of God's Kingdom since the time of Jesus. One of the greatest of these was a man who told of the love of Jesus and helped set up churches. After he continued on his trips he would write letters to these new churches, telling them how to be better followers of Jesus.

since	prince	produce	officer	once
chance	france	advance	except	
dance	distance	dancer	difference	

Lesson 95

 general

 village

1 | general
ge

3 | general
gentleman

5 | german
germany

1 | village
ge

3 | village
college

5 | trenton
princeton

5 |
age	george
angel	judge
bridge	judgment
change	large
charge	page
edge	strange
danger	stranger
orange	wage
manage	manager

general gentleman george german germany village
college strange age angel bridge change charge
edge judge judgment large page

A general is one of the most important men in an army. General George Washington was a gentleman who is judged important to the history of this country. Over two hundred years ago, he helped this country win its freedom.

The enemy had sent a large army of men from Germany to take charge. Most of the men were housed in the village of Trenton. General Washington decided to take his army and cross a river to get to Trenton. There was no bridge over the river, so he had to find boats for all his men. When he reached the edge of the village he found most of the Germans were asleep. His own men were able to take charge of Trenton without much of a battle.

Washington's good judgment had helped his men win for a change. Later, they won another battle near the college town of Princeton. However, it took years of battles before this would be a free country.

✠ Strange things will take place at the end of this age. Before the Day of Judgment comes there will be a great battle between the followers of Jesus and the followers of the Devil, that angel of darkness. Jesus will be our general and we will defeat the forces of the Devil for all time. This is the way the last page in the history of the Earth will end.

page   general   large   gentleman   judgment   george
judge   german   edge   germany   charge   village   change
college   bridge   strange   angel   age

Lesson 96

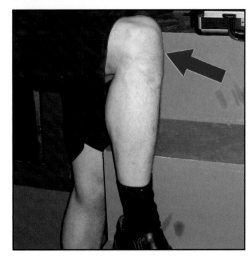

knee

sign

1　knee
　　ee

2　ee　　own　　eel
　　knee　known　kneel

3　knee
　　known
　　kneel

5　knew　　knock
　　knife　　know

1　gnat
　　at

1　foreign
　　eign

1　gnaw
　　aw

3　gnat
　　gnaw

　　sign
　　foreign

5　disease

knee　known　kneel　knew　knife
knock　know　gnaw　sign　foreign

I once knew an old man who could always tell what kind of weather we were going to have. When I asked him how he could know that a storm or snow was coming, he would point to his knee. "When I get a little pain that gnaws at my joints," he said, "it is a sign that we are going to have a change of weather. A bigger pain means the weather will be bad. When I get a pain like a knife that is so bad I can't even kneel down, then it's been known to rain for four days in a row or pile up snow three feet deep."

✝ One day, as Jesus was going into a village, he was met by ten men who had a bad skin disease. They stood at a distance and shouted, "Jesus, Master, help us!"

When Jesus saw them, he said to them, "Go and let the leaders at the house of God look at you." While they were going, they became well. When one of them saw he was well he turned back and shouted praises to God. Then he bowed down to the ground at Jesus' feet and thanked him. The man was from a foreign country.

Jesus asked of those around him, "Weren't there ten men made well? Where are the other nine? Why is this foreigner the only one to come back and priase God?" Then Jesus said to the man, "Get up and go. You were made well because you trust in me."

foreign	knee	sign	known	gnaw
kneel	know	knew	knock	knife

Lesson 97

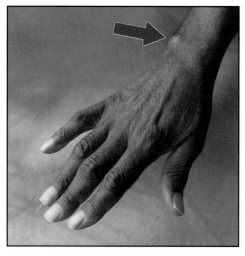

wrist

lamb

1 | wrist
rist

5 | answer   write
sword   written
whole   writer
wrap   wrong
wreck   wrote

1 | lamb
lam

5 | climb   doubt
comb   dumb
debt   thumb

wrist   answer   whole   wrap   wreck   write   written
writer   wrong   lamb   climb   debt   doubt   dumb   thumb

My oldest brother, James, ran away from home two months ago. He didn't write us until last week. His letter said, "Dear Mom and Dad, I knew it was wrong not to have written to you sooner, but you know I have never been much of a writer. Besides that, I broke my wrist six weeks ago and the doctor had it all wrapped up. It was hurt in a car wreck. I had been thumbing rides across the country, and I was rather dumb. I have no doubt now that climbing in the car with someone who had been drinking was a bad idea. But it was very cold, few cars were passing, and I hadn't had a thing to eat for a whole day. Well, it was a bad wreck, but I'm fine now.

I have been helping a fellow care for his sheep. The work is not bad, but I am tired of eating lamb all the time.

I would like to come back home. I need some money to get out of debt. Could you send me a hundred dollars? I will wait for an answer. Love, James."

✝ In the time of Jesus, men who had sinned would give lambs, cows, and birds to God. They would place parts of these animals in a fire. The smoke was supposed to rise up to God. He would smell the burning meat and forgive the man's sin. At least this is what they hoped would happen.

It is a fact, however, that all men are so full of sin that their debt to God could never be repaid. So Jesus was sent to die on the cross to pay off the sins of men once and for all.

He is the Lamb who has been offered to save us from sin. If we live in sin we will die and never have a chance to live in Heaven. If we let the blood of Jesus wash away our sins, and follow Jesus as our Lord, we will be raised to life everlasting on Judgment Day.

thumb   wrist   dumb   answer   doubt   whole   debt   wrap
climb   wreck   lamb   write   wrong   written   writer

225

Lesson 98

calf

john

1
| calf |
| caf |

5
| half |
| talk |
| walk |

1
| john |
| jon |

5
ghost	oh
honest	school
honor	thomas
hour	

calf   half   talk   walk   john   ghost
honest   honor   hour   oh   school   thomas

"Where were you all morning?" Mary Thomas said crossly to her husband, Ben. "I needed you to help me lift some heavy things in the living room, so I could clean there for once."

"Oh, I just took a walk over to John Singer's place," Ben answered. "I honestly didn't think I would be gone more than half an hour. But you know John. Once he starts to talk you can never get away. First he had to show me his new calf and tell me all the trouble he has had with it. The poor little thing looks rather sickly, and I don't think it will last out the week. Then he had to tell me about the honor roll his son Tim is on at school. The boy is number one in his class, so his father has good reason to be proud of him. Finally, he spent about an hour telling me about a ghost he saw over in the old Jackson house. He may think it was a ghost, but if you ask me I would bet it was someone playing a trick on old John."

One evening the followers of Jesus went out on the lake in a boat. When they were three or four miles from shore a storm came up that kept their boat from reaching the shore. When it was almost morning the men saw Jesus coming toward them, walking on the water. They were afraid, thinking it was a ghost. Jesus spoke to them, "Be glad! It is I. Do not fear."

His follower, Peter, said, "Lord, if it is you, tell me to come to you on the water." When Jeus told him to come, Peter walked on the water toward Jesus. However, the waves and wind made him afraid and he began to sink into the water. "Lord, save me!" he called out. Jesus put out his hand and held him up.

When they both got into the boat the wind stopped blowing. The men in the boat bowed down in front of Jesus. "You are really the Son of God!" they said.

| thomas | calf | school | half | oh | talk |
| hour | walk | honor | john | honest | ghost |

227

Lesson 99

 castle

 clothes

1 castle
  casle

5 christmas   often
  fasten   soften
  listen   whistle
  mustn't

1 clothes   1 muscle   5 scene
  cloes   musle   scissors

5 herd
  shepherd

castle christmas fasten listen mustn't often
whistle clothes muscle scene scissors

Our church has a play each year on the Sunday before Christmas. Mrs. Peg Castle is always in charge of it. For a month in advance, she and the other ladies have been at work making clothes with their scissors, needles, and thread.

If you listen closely, you can hear Mrs. Walker whistle as she works. She is such a happy person and will often sing a little song to help make the others happy too.

Do you hear that hammering? Come this way and you will see the boys at work. Watch out! You mustn't trip over the wood and tools on the floor. The boys will fasten the wood together and make a big frame. Some of the girls are painting a scene on old bed sheets which will be hung on the frame. That frame is heavy. It will take a lot of muscle to put it into place. However, everyone is so pleased with the play each year that all the work is worth it.

You know that our Lord Jesus was not born in a king's castle. When he was born on Christmas Day it was in a stable where cows, sheep, and horses lived. The first persons who came to worship him were shepherds. Angels had told them of the birth of this baby who would bring news of God's Kingdom and save men from sin.

When Jesus grew up and began to preach he often called himself a shepherd. He said, "I am the Good Shepherd. I know my sheep and my sheep know me. I am willing to die to save these sheep. I have other sheep which are not in this sheep pen. I must bring them also. They will listen to my voice and be one herd with one shepherd."

Will you let Jesus be the shepherd who will keep you safe from sin?

scissors   castle   scene   christmas   muscle   fasten
clothes   listen   whistle   mustn't   often

Lesson 100

daughter

knight

1
daughter
dauter

3
caught
fought
taught

5
bought	height	ought	slight
bright	knight	right	fright
brought	light	sight	frighten
fight	might	straight	brighten
high	night	thought	thoughtless

5
although
thoroughly
though

5 through

5
wagon
dragon
dragonfly

230
daughter caught fought taught bought bright brought fight
high height knight light might night ought right sight
straight thought although throughly though through

"Will you tell me a story when you are through reading?" my daughter Jennie asked. "I might do it right now," I said, "even though I am not finished with the paper. It is rather late at night for you to be up, though. So, after the story, you ought to go straight to bed. Do you want me to read that new book I brought home last week? You know, the one I bought at the market." "No," said Jennie. "I thought you might just tell me a story, one of the ones you make up as you go along." Although I would rather have read to her, I began a story.

"Once there was a knight who had never been taught to fight. He lived high up on a hill in his castle. From that height all of the country for miles around could be kept in sight. One day as he watched from his castle wall, the knight saw that a bright green dragon had just caught a little girl. As dragons do, he took her off to his cave. There he would keep her until a knight fought for her. Our poor knight was thoroughly upset. He knew he would be expected to save the girl, but he had never fought anyone before. So he thought and thought. At last he had an idea. First he went out and bought some taffy candy. Then he dug a deep hole and covered it over with branches and leaves. Finally, he very carefully dropped bits of taffy on the ground between the hole and the dragon's cave. When the dragon came out he picked up the bits and ate them, getting his jaws all stuck together. But he loved taffy candy, so he went on picking it up until he fell into the hole. Now the knight could save the girl, for the dragon could not get out of the hole. With his jaws stuck he couldn't even shoot fire from his mouth. So the girl was saved and the knight went back to his castle."

"But what happened to the dragon?" asked Jennie. "Oh," I said, "he didn't have anything to eat for a long time. He got smaller and smaller and smaller. Finally, he became a dragonfly and flew away."

✝ One of the followers of Jesus was a man named John. He wrote a book about Jesus. In that book Jesus tells us about himself. What he tells us are called the seven great "I Am's." We have seen that he said, "I am the vine," "I am the Bread of Life," and "I am the Good Shepherd." He also told us, "I am the Light of the World." By this he means, "I am the one who can push back the darkness of sin in this world. I can let you see the path to the Kingdom of God."

through daughter though caught thoroughly fought although taught thought bought straight bright sight brought right fight ought high night height might knight light

231

Lesson 101

 laugh

 woman

3 | laugh
tough
enough

5 | cough
rough

3 | could
should
would

5 | your
yourself
yourselves

3 | woman
wolf

5 | dave
david

laugh tough enough cough rough
could should would woman wolf

"Yes," the old woman said to my mom with a bitter laugh, "life has been rough for me since George passed away. Times are tough enough for somone with a job these days. But for a widow who has to live on her monthly check, there never seems to be enough to keep the wolf from the door. Now I have this bad cough. I know I should go to the doctor, but where would I get the money to pay him? Can you tell me where I could go to get some help."

As Jesus and his followers left one city, a crowd came along with them. A blind man was sitting by the side of the road, begging for money. When he heard that Jesus was passing he shouted, "Jesus, Son of David! Help me!" Those who were with Jesus told him to be still, but he only shouted louder, "Son of David! Help me!"

Jesus stopped and said, "Call him." So they called the blind man and said to him, "Be glad! Come along! Jesus is calling for you." The man threw off his coat, jumped up, and went to Jesus. Jesus asked him, "What do you want me to do for you?" The blind man answered, "Teacher, I want to see."

Jesus said, "Go home. You will have your sight because you came to me in trust." At that moment, the man was able to see for the first time. He then followed Jesus down the road, giving thanks to God. When the crowd saw what happened, they all praised God.

wolf	laugh	woman	tough	would
enough	should	cough	could	rough

233

Lesson 102

movie

shoe

1 movie
   o

3 do
   two
   who

5 lose   prove
   move   whom
   movement   whose

5 shoe
   canoe

movie   do   two   who   canoe   move
movement   prove   shoe   whom   whose

I saw a movie on TV the other day that I liked a whole lot. It was about two men who took a long canoe trip on a very wild river. Why did they do it? They said they had to prove something.

I saw them move that canoe through some rough water that was full of rocks. In some places a movement that was only slightly wrong would send them into the water. The canoe did turn over once and I saw one of the men lose a shoe. They did manage to get back in, though, and continue their trip.

I can't recall whose idea it was to start the trip, but I know both men were glad when it was finished. I also think they did prove something. They proved to me that they were crazy!

✝ Jesus is the one whom we can trust in any time of danger. He proved that to his followers, and he has proven it since then to those who have called on him for help.

One day, Jesus was in a boat with his men. After Jesus went to sleep, a strong wind blew down on the lake. The boat began to fill with water, and his men were very frightened. They ran to Jesus and woke him.

"Master, Master!" they cried. "We are about to die!" Jesus said to them, "Why do you fear? You do not trust in God's power very much!" Then he got up and said to the wind and waves, "Stop!" Then all became still. His followers were surprised and said to each other, "What kind of man is this to whom even the wind and waves listen?"

| whose | movie | whom | do | shoe | two |
| prove | who | movement | canoe | move | |

235

Lesson 103

 fruit

 soup

3 | fruit
juice
suit |

3 | soup
group
wounded |

3 | view
review |

3 | beauty
beautiful |

236

| fruit juice suit soup group
wounded view beauty beautiful |

Ted Wagoner took my older sister, Katy, out to dinner last night. He was wearing his new suit, and she had on a long, green dress. They went to a place called the Red River House. I hear it has a beautiful view of the river and the food is very good.

Poor Ted always seems to have problems though. They had just finished some fruit juice when the waiter brought their soup. He tripped over a chair leg and the whole tray fell on Ted. One of the glasses broke and wounded Ted's left hand. It was a real beauty of a cut.

Ted did have one good thing happen. There was a doctor in the group that was eating at the Red River House that night. The doctor was able to fix Ted's wound.

✝ The Lord's Day was the day when everyone in the time of Jesus went to the meeting house to praise God. It was the law that a man could not do any kind of work at all on the Lord's Day. Jesus was in a meeting house teaching on one of these days. A man was there whose right hand was thin and weak. The enemies of Jesus were watching to see if he would heal this man on the Lord's Day. They wanted to find something wrong with Jesus. Jesus knew what was in their evil minds.

He spoke to the man whose hand was thin and weak and said, "Come and stand here in front." Then Jesus said to the group, "I ask you, is it right to do good things on the Lord's Day, or to do bad things? Should we heal others so they will live, or should we let them die?" After he looked around at them all, he said to the man, "Hold out your hand." The man did as he was told and the hand was made well just like the other. The enemies of Jesus were mad at Jesus for doing this and began to plan what they could do to him.

beautiful	fruit	beauty	juice	view
suit	wounded	soup	group	

Lesson 104

 building

 women

1 | building
uil

3 | building
build
built

5 | business
busy
minute

1 | system
y

1 | hymn
y

3 | hymn
system

1 | women
o

1 | pretty
e

building   build   built   business   busy
minute   system   women   pretty

The new church building on the corner was built by Ben Cousins' company. My older brother, Jack, works for Mr. Cousins. He told me that you can be busy every minute in that business.

Mr. Cousins is trying out a new system. He says that by using it he will be able to put up a house five times faster. How does he do that? Most of the parts of the house are made in another place and are brought to the lot by truck. That seems like a pretty good idea to me. I never liked to see rain and snow falling on an unfinished house. With Mr. Cousins' system a house will be put up so fast that the weather will not have a chance to hurt it.

Women were not treated very kindly in the time of Jesus. If a husband did not like his wife, he could be rid of her just by sending her away. If a woman was unfaithful to her husband, she could be killed. The husband, on the other hand, was free to do just about as he pleased.

One day, Jesus was talking to the crowd. His enemies brought a woman to him. "Teacher," they said, "we caught this woman sleeping with a man who is not her husband. Our law tells us that a woman who does this should be killed with stones. What do you say?" They were trying to get Jesus to say something wrong, so they could charge him with breaking the law. However, Jesus just bent down and wrote on the ground.

When they kept on asking him, he stood up and said, "The one among you who has never sinned may hit her with the first stone." Then he bent down once more and wrote on the ground. When the men heard what he said, they left, one by one. The oldest ones left first. At last Jesus was left alone with the woman. He looked up and said to her, "Woman, where is everyone? Is there no one left to judge you?"

"There is no one, sir," she answered. "Well then," Jesus said, "I do not judge you. You may leave, but do not sin anymore."

pretty   building   women   build   system
built   minute   business   busy

Lesson 105

chief

people

1 | chief
ie

2 | ie   ie   ie
chief   niece   field

3 | chief
niece
field

1 | either
ei

3 | either
neither
receive

4 | believe   niece   piece
receive   neither   either

5 | pierce
fierce

1 | people
eo

5 | baptize
cupboard

5 | hole
holy

chief   niece   field   believe   fierce
piece   either   neither   receive   people

Bill Pierce's niece, Mary, was sent by our church to South America. She helps teach the people in one tribe about Jesus. Until a few years ago, this fierce tribe was only interested in killing its enemies and taking their heads. Now most of the people believe in the Good News of Jesus. The chief even gave a piece of one of his fields on which to build a church.

There is a real problem that Mary has, however. Neither the chief nor any of the others in the tribe can read. Until they learn to read, they can only receive the Good News from Mary. After they can read, though, they will be able to let the Word of God speak to them.

Just before Jesus was taken up into Heaven, he stood on a hill with his 11 followers. Jesus said to them, "All power in Heaven and on earth has been given to me. So go and find more followers for me in all countries. Baptize them in the name of the Father, and of the Son, and of the Holy Spirit. Teach them to do all the things I have told you to do. The one who believes the Good News and is baptized will be saved. Anyone who does not believe will be judged and dropped into the lake of fire. I will be with you always even to the end of the world."

After Jesus spoke to them he was taken up into Heaven. A cloud carried him away so they could not see him. As his followers were watching him go, two men dressed in white stood beside them. These men said, "Why do you stand looking up into Heaven? This same Jesus who was taken from you into Heaven will return in the same way you saw him go up into Heaven."

If we are followers of Jesus we must do as he commands. We can either go to other countries to spread the Good News or we can help send others. Even if we stay right in our hometown, we can tell others about Jesus and the path to God's Kingdom.

| people | chief | receive | niece | neither |
| field | either | believe | piece | fierce |

241

Lesson 106

friend

guest

1 friend
   ie

3 friend
   friendly
   friendship

3 again
   against
   said

3 guest
   guess

3 any
   many
   busy
   pantry
   hungry
   angry

5 any
   anything
   anyone

5 sorry
   sorrow
   borrow

friend   friendship   again   against   said
guest   guess   any   anything   many

"I have a friend coming tomorrow," said Mrs. Johnson. "Our friendship goes back many years to the days when we were in school. It will be so nice to have her as a guest again. She said that she would be here Friday on the nine a.m. train. I guess I should check the pantry and be certain we are not out of any kind of food. If we are, I will call my husband and he can pick up anything I need on his way home."

✝ Jesus was often a guest in the homes of tax men and others who were considered to be sinners. His enemies were very much against this and told him so.

So, Jesus told them this story. "What if one of you had one hundred sheep and lost one of them? Wouldn't you leave the 99 in the field and go back to look for the one you had lost? And when you find it, wouldn't you be so happy that you would carry it back? Then you would go to your house and call in your friends. You would say, 'Be happy with me because I have found the sheep that was lost.'

In the same way, if a woman has ten silver coins and loses one, what does she do? Doesn't she light a lamp and sweep the floor and look until she finds it? When she finds it she will call to her friends, 'Be happy with me for I have found the coin I had lost.' I tell you, there is more joy in Heaven for one sinner who is sorry for his sins and turns from them, than for all the others who do not have sins to be sorry for."

| many | friend | anything | friendship | any |
| again | guess | against | guest | said |

Lesson 107

neighbor

shoulder

1 neighbor
   ei

3 neighbor
   eight
   weight

1 they
   ey

3 they
   obey
   grey

1 shoulder
   oul

3 soul
   shoulder
   boulder

neighbor   eight   weight   they
obey   grey   shoulder   soul

My neighbor, Mrs. Grey, has eight children. She says that they are not as much trouble as you might think. They all have been taught to obey, and the older children help to take care of the younger. I am certain this takes a great weight off Mrs. Grey's shoulders. I know some families where the children just run wild.

✝ Jesus told many stories to the crowds to try to teach them important lessons. The story of the lost son was told to show God's happiness when a lost soul returns to the right path. Jesus began the story in this way, "There was once a man who had two sons. One day the younger son asked for the part of the family riches which would be his. So his father shared all he owned between his two sons. The younger one took all that he was given and went off to a far country and spent the money foolishly. When his money was gone he was hungry. He finally got a job feeding pigs, but he was still so hungry that he wanted to eat the food that the pigs were given. He began to think how foolish he was. His father had many men who worked for him. None of them ever went hungry.

So the son decided to go home and tell his father, 'Father, I have sinned against heaven and against you. I am not good enough to be called your son. But please let me be one of your workmen.' As the son came near his old home, his father saw him and was filled with loving pity for him. He ran to him and threw his arms around him.

Then he called to his men, 'Hurry! Get the best coat and put it on him. Put a ring on his hand and shoes on his feet. Bring the fat calf and kill it. Let us eat and be glad. For my son was dead and is now alive again. He was lost and has now been found.'

When the older brother heard this he was angry. He did not think his brother deserved such good treatment. But his father told him, 'Son, you are with me all the time and all that I have is yours. But it is right for us to have a good time and be glad. Your brother was dead and is now alive. He was lost and now is found.'"

soul   neighbor   shoulder   eight
grey   weight   obey   they

245

Lesson 108

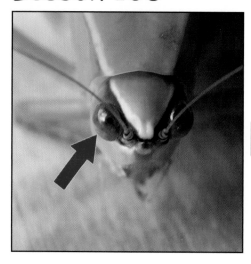 eye

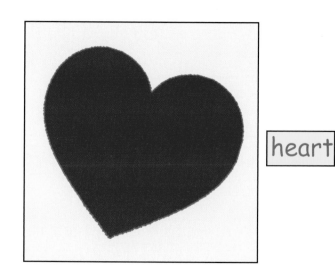 heart

3 | eye
eyebrow

3 | buy
guy

5 | guide

5 | island

5 | guard

5 | heart

eye eyebrow buy guy
guide island guard heart

Mr. Benson raised one eyebrow. "You are going to buy an island?" he said in a surprised voice. "Yes," said his son, Guy, looking him right in the eye. "It's a small island that no one lives on. I think that old Captain Blackbeard hid some of his gold there. I found a map that will help guide me to the right place. Will you come along and guard all the money for me?"

"Of course," said Mr. Benson. He didn't have the heart to tell Guy that he had drawn the map many years before. Besides, why spoil an eight-year-old boy's dream?

✚ Jesus spoke many times about the Kingdom of Heaven. Each time he said it was like something different. In this way we can come to know a bit more about the Kingdom.

Jesus said, "The Kingdom of Heaven is like a box of gold hidden in a field. A man happens to find it, so he covers it up again. In his joy he goes and sells everything he has. Then he goes back and buys the field."

"The Kingdom of Heaven is also like a buyer looking for pearls. At last he finds one that is worth a great deal of money. So he goes home and sells everything that he owns. Then he returns and buys the one fine pearl. He will guard it with his life."

| heart | eye | guard | eyebrow |
| island | buy | guide | guy |

247

Lesson 109

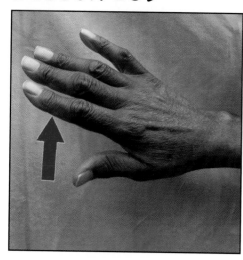

finger

onion

3 | finger
longer
single

5 | hunger
hungry

5 | england
english

5 | london
british
europe

3 | onion
million
companion

5 | opinion

1 | period
i

3 | period
indian
glorious

finger   longer   single   england   english   london   british
248   europe   onion   million   companion   period   indian   glorious

"See, Helen," said Mrs. Johns, pointing with her finger. "There is that ad in the paper I told you about. 'Fly now, pay later,' it says. 'A trip to London, England and seven other countries in Europe.' Look, you can stay for one week, two weeks, or even longer. I'm sure that Peg would go as your traveling companion, and you will meet just millions of single men. I think British men are so nice. It would be such a glorious trip for you to take."

"Slow down please, Mother," her oldest daughter broke in, "I am not going to England, period! Why my friend, Mary, was there and says the English food is really bad. She ordered some onion soup and they even burned that. The only time she got good food was in one little Indian place. I don't care how many single men are there if I am going to die of hunger."

✝ Getting into heaven is like the great wedding dinner a king had prepared for his son. Many people had been asked to the wedding, but when the king sent his servants to call them, they would not come. They all had their own reasons. One said, "I bought a field and have to go look at it." Another said, "I bought 5 pairs of oxen and am on my way to try them out." A third told the king that he had just gotten married himself.

The king was very angry and said to his servants, "Go out to the back streets of the city. Bring here all the people who are poor, hurt, blind, or lame." The servants came back and reported, "Sir, we have done this and there is still room left for more people." So the King said, "Go out to the country roads and paths and make everyone come to fill up my house. But none of those men who were invited at first will get to eat any of this dinner."

glorious	finger	companion	longer	million	single	onion
england	europe	english	british	london	indian	period

Lesson 110

sugar

ocean

3 sugar
sure

5 issue

3 ocean
especially
special

3 chicago
machine

sugar   sure   issue   ocean
especially   special   chicago   machine

My uncle, Mike, lives in Chicago. He works down at the docks unloading the big ships that come in. Some of them have traveled across the ocean. They come to Chicago after an especially long trip on rivers and lakes. What do these ships bring? They carry oil, coal, bags of sugar, and boxes filled with all sorts of special things.

There is a real problem at issue on the docks these days. The owners want to put in more machines and have fewer men working. The men who work with Uncle Mike do not want them to do this. They are afraid that they will lose their jobs. My uncle says that there is sure to be a strike if more machines are brought in. Then nobody will be working!

✝ Jesus spoke again about the Kingdom of Heaven. He said, "It is like the owner of a farm who went out early in the morning to look for men to work on his land. He agreed to pay them a fair wage, which was one silver coin a day. A few hours later he went out again. He saw some men standing around at the market doing nothing. So he said to them, 'You go out to work on my farm and I will pay you what is right.' The man again went out at noon, at three, and at five and hired more workers.

When the evening came, the farm owner had his manager call in all the workers to be paid. First he gave a silver coin to the men who had started at five. When the others saw this they were sure that they would be paid more, but everyone was paid just one silver coin. The ones who had worked all day were very angry at the farm owner. 'We did all the work in the hot sun,' they said, 'and you are only giving us as much as those who worked one hour!'

The farm owner said to them, 'My friends, I am not hurting you. You agreed that I should pay you a silver coin, didn't you? Take your money and go. If I want to give the last man the same as you, it is my money. Is it a bad thing for me to be especially kind?'"

"In the same way," Jesus said, "the people who are now last will be first and those who are first will be last."

| machine | sugar | chicago | sure |
| special | issue | especially | ocean |

251

Lesson 111

station

treasure

1 station
   tion

3 station
   action
   motion

5 condition   nation
   position   national

3 treasure
   pleasure
   measure

5 usual
   usually

station   action   motion   condition   position   nation
national   treasure   pleasure   measure   usual   usually

252

Dad was talking to Mom about how the old railroad station is in bad condition these days. The National Railroad doesn't stop there anymore and the station has nothing in it except for rats, bats, and birds. He said that as usual when something like this happens, it took awhile before any action was taken. However, last week at the town meeting, Uncle Bill made a motion to have the station taken down.

Dad said that before this measure could be acted on, Mrs. Johnson jumped up and demanded that money be found to fix up the old building as a children's play center. She said that the station was a "real treaure," one of the oldest of its kind in the nation. As a play center it would provide a lot of pleasure for the children of our town.

Now Mrs. Johnson usually gets her way when she speaks up strongly. However, a lot of people agree with Uncle Bill's position. It would cost a lot less to tear down the station than to repair it.

✝ Jesus told the crowds, "Everyone who hears these words of mine and follows them will be like the wise man who built his house on a rock. The rain came down and the water rose. The wind blew and hit the house. But the house did not fall because it was built on a rock. Whoever hears these words and does not follow them will be like the foolish man who built his house on sand. The rain came down and the water rose. The wind blew and hit the house. And that house fell and broke apart, because it was built on sand."

We must always ask, "What condition is our life in? Is it built on the rock of God's plan? Or are we in the position of the foolish man who has a life that rests on the moving sands of the Devil's promises?"

usually	station	usual	action	measure	motion
pleasure	condition	treasure	position	national	nation

Lesson 112

picture

soldier

3 picture
   future
   century

5 nature   question
   natural

3 soldier
   education
   gradually

5 direct
   direction
   attention

5 haul
   paul
   saul

picture future century nature natural question
      soldier education gradually direct direction

This is a picture of my friend, Steve. He is a soldier in the army. Steve did not finish high school before he went into the service. Now he is gradually finishing his education at night. My mother says that Steve never was given much direction at home, so it was natural for him to just slowly move along through life. The army has forced him to direct some attention to his future. He has come to question the nature of his past actions. Is there a place for him? Will he get there without a great deal of work? The army is training Steve as a cook. This may be the work he will really do well in. Mom says at least now he has a chance to find out.

✝ Paul was one of the greatest followers of Jesus. He lived in the first century after Jesus was taken up to Heaven. He wrote many letters to the new churches. Some of these letters answered questions people had about Jesus. Others were written to direct the people away from the path of the Devil.

Paul said in one letter that the church is the body of Jesus Christ. God has chosen different ones in the church to do his work. Paul tells us that each part of the body is important. The eye cannot say to the hand, "I do not need you," or the head cannot say to the feet, "I do not need you." In the same way we all have a part to play in God's church. Some of us are preachers and some are teachers. One may heal the sick and another may go to foreign lands to tell of Jesus. Each of us has an important part to play as one member of the body of Christ. We should not be so proud of our own part, however, that we look down on the one someone else has.

direction   picture   direct   future   gradually   century
education   nature   soldier   natural   question

255

Lesson 113

president

value

5 | president

5 | object
subject

5 | success

5 | supply
reply

5 | value

5 | visit

5 | various

5 | government

5 | public
panic

5 | vote
rome

5 | punish
punishment

president   object   subject   success   supply
reply   value   various   government

Our teacher told us that the president is the man we pick every four years to rule all the people in the country. He is the one who must supply us with good direction and leadership. If he is a wise president he can be of great value to the country. However, if too many people object to the way he runs the government he will have no success. Instead, he will subject the country to a great many problems. This has happened at various times in the past century. Three of the presidents were almost removed from their job. Another died before any action was taken against him.

The president is certainly the most powerful man in the country. Each one of us, though, has the right to reply to what he says or does. We can write letters to his office, we can talk to other people about him, or we can wait for four years and vote for the man who is running against him.

Our teacher says that in many other countries it would not be possible to do any of these things. In these countries, men are often put in jail for saying something against the government.

Paul wrote one of his letters to the church in Rome. He told them, "Every person must obey the rulers who are over him. Every ruler was put there by God and has his power from God. The rulers do not bring fear to a good man, but they do bring fear to a bad man. If you do not want to be afraid of a ruler, do what is good and he will praise you for it. The ruler works for God to do what is good for you. But he will punish a person who does what is wrong, and God is also angry with that person. So you must obey, not only because God will be angry with you, but because you know it is right. That is why you also pay taxes. The rulers work for God and give all their time to this work. So pay them all they should have. Pay taxes to the people who should have taxes. Respect the people who should be respected, and honor those who should be honored."

government	president	various	object	value
subject	reply	success	supply	

Lesson 114

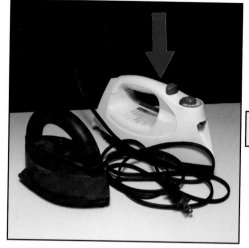 modern

 resurrection

5 modern

5 accept
   attempt

5 bible

5 complete
   control

5 effort

5 regard

5 resurrection

258

modern   accept   attempt   complete
control   effort   regard   resurrection

✝ In this modern age there are many who are looking for "truth," for "peace," or for "some meaning to life." Some have even made an effort to control their future by dealing with the Devil and the other dark powers. All of their attempts, however, have failed in the past, and we can regard it as certain that none of them will work in the future.

The only way to find "truth, peace, and meaning" in this life is to accept the Lord Jesus as your guide. He is the complete and final answer to all of your questions. Jesus said, "I am the Resurrection and the Life. The person who believes in me will live, even though he has died. Anyone who is living and who believes in me will never die."

Will you allow Jesus to save you from a life of sin? Will you accept the promise of the resurrection and the life in God's Kingdom? Ask Jesus to come into your heart right now! Read the Bible yourself and discover the path to God's Kingdom. The Bible is now an open book for you, because you have learned to read.

| resurrection | modern | accept | regard |
| attempt | effort | complete | control |

Would you like to invite Jesus into your heart right now
and make him Lord of your life?
You may use the following prayer as a guide:

Dear God,
I know that I am a sinner and my sins
keep me separated from you forever.
I believe that Jesus Christ died
for my sins and rose again.
I ask Jesus to be Lord of my life
and place my trust in him alone.
Thank you for your forgiveness and
the gift of eternal life with you in Heaven.
Amen

Now that you have trusted Christ as your Savior,
you will want to grow in your relationship with him
through prayer, reading the Bible daily, and
worshiping with God's people in a local church.
Be sure to tell someone about your decision to follow Jesus.

We would love to hear from you or your tutor!
Christian Literacy Associates
541 Perry Highway
Pittsburgh, PA 15229
412-364-3777
E-mail: drliteracy@aol.com
www.christianliteracy.com

The Christian Literacy Series